About the Book

Can you find the Big Dipper? What about Leo, the Lion; Aquarius, the Water Carrier; or the other constellations in the zodiac?

With Melvin Berger's clear and informative text and monthly star charts, now you can spot these constellations in the night sky, recognize their imaginary shapes, their positions each month, their brightest stars, and even discover the myths behind their appearances.

And there's more: You can learn how to spot comets, observe and record meteor showers, build an astrolabe to make your own map of the sky, and even plot the progress of Halley's Comet so you won't miss its return.

Through simple experiments and activities, here's a fun-filled opportunity for *you* to be the astronomer.

STAR GAZING, COMET TRACKING and SKY MAPPING

MELVIN BERGER

illustrations by William Negron

G. P. PUTNAM'S SONS / New York

Photo Credits
American Meteorite Laboratory, p. 61 · Celestron International, p. 6
Harvard College Observatory, p. 57 · NASA, p. 48 · The Science Museum, p. 54
Cover photograph of the Andromeda Galaxy and photograph on page 2
of the Pleiades, courtesy Celestron International

*The author wishes to thank Captain William McMullen,
Associate Academic Dean, Nautical Science Department, U.S. Merchant
Marine Academy, Kings Point, New York, for reading this text.*

 Published simultaneously in
Canada by General Publishing Co. Limited, Toronto.
Printed in the United States of America
Second Impression
Book design by Virginia Evans

Library of Congress Cataloging in Publication Data
Berger, Melvin.
Star gazing, comet tracking, and sky mapping.
Bibliography: p.
Includes index.
Summary: Explains how to learn about stars, constellations, comets, and other astronomical phenomena by studying the sky without a telescope.
1. Astronomy—Observers' manuals—Juvenile literature.
[1. Astronomy—Observers' manuals. 2. Stars. 3. Constellations. 4. Comets. 5. Sky] I. Title.
QB64.B47 1985 523 84-8302
ISBN 0-399-61211-4

Contents

An exciting view of the stars as seen in the night sky.

1 / Star Gazing

On any night of the year, you can see a most thrilling show—just by looking up at the stars in the night sky.

On clear, dark nights, you can count up to 3,000 separate stars—without a telescope! You are able to see stars that are trillions of miles out in space. Their light has been traveling for hundreds or thousands of years before reaching earth.

You can enjoy the wonder of the skies in much the same way people have from earliest times. You can watch the stars come out. You can see the special patterns, called constellations, that they form in the sky. You can watch them move from month to month. You can use them to find your direction. You can even tell time by the sky, and keep track of the seasons.

During the day, you see only one star, the sun. The sun rises in the east, crosses the sky and then sets in the west. Although there are many other stars in the day sky, you cannot see them because the sky is too light. But as the sun sets, the sky darkens. You begin to see the brightest stars first. As the sky gets darker, more stars become visible, and you will feel the same sense of excitement that humans have always felt as they gazed at those wondrous objects.

Finding the Constellations

When ancient stargazers looked up at the nighttime sky, they created pictures by drawing imaginary lines connecting the bright stars. They called these pictures constellations. And they named the constellations after gods, people, animals and objects. Most of the names and legends were based on the myths of ancient Greece and Rome.

If you live in or near a big city, you may not be able to see all the stars the ancients did. The glow of city lights brightens the sky and makes it harder to see the less brilliant stars. Yet, in a way, you may find it easier to spot constellations since the landmark bright stars that they contain stand out vividly. If you are a country person, you will see many more stars, and the great number of dim stars may confuse things a bit at first. But, in time, they will make the discovery process all the more amazing.

Some of the pictures that people found in the sky long ago are easy to see. Orion, the Hunter, is an example of such a constellation. People in several different cultures around the world have come up with similar pictures of a powerful giant with a bright belt for that part of the sky.

Other constellations, though, bear no resemblance to the names people gave them. Take Perseus, the Hero, for example: The stars do not really have the shape of a brave young man. These constellation names were just a way to honor or recall some mythical or legendary character.

Even though some constellations do not look like particular figures, they have become associated with certain names and shapes. Getting to know these pictures and the legends surrounding them will make it easier for you to find the constellations and their main stars.

Altogether there are eighty-eight constellations. No one can see all of them. Some are in the southern skies and can be seen only from the Southern Hemisphere; people north of the equator never see these constellations. Others are visible only to people living in the Northern Hemisphere.

Also, the positions of the constellations change as the earth moves through space. The earth makes one orbit around the sun every year, and the constellations you can see during any month depend on the earth's position in relation to the sun. Because of this, the constellations appear to be moving through the sky, month by month. The whole sky seems to turn slowly to the west during the year. After a full year, the stars are back in the same positions as a year earlier, and the cycle is complete.

Some constellations can be seen all year long. Most can be seen only during several months. Yet there is one month of the year in which a constellation can be seen most readily. During that month, the constellation is either at its highest point or is shining most brightly. This is known as the culminating position. In this book, the constellations are presented in the order in which they reach their culminating position, from January to December.

We will focus on thirty constellations that are visible from nearly anywhere in the United States. This includes the twelve constellations—Taurus, Gemini, Cancer, Leo, Virgo, Libra, Scorpius, Sagittarius, Capricornus, Aquarius, Pisces, Aries—that make up the zodiac. The zodiac, which means "circle of animals," is an imaginary belt stretching across the sky through which the planets travel. It is usually divided into twelve equal sections called the signs of the zodiac; each section is named after the constellation found there.

Using Star Charts

Star charts are maps that help you to recognize the stars and constellations. Most, but not all, are circular in shape. They show the bright stars as though they were being projected on the inside of a giant, upside-down soup bowl. Each star chart shows only the stars that are visible in a single hemisphere. Since the earth's orbit makes it seem that the constellations are always moving, a star chart for May looks different from one for June. Some stars that weren't there in May will appear in June. And just about every star will be in a different position.

The twelve star charts included in this section show the night sky as it appears during each month of the year. More exactly, they picture the sky as it looks on the 16th day of the month at 9:00 P.M. They are also drawn to show the view you get from latitude 40° north. This is an imaginary line that runs east to west across the United States. It passes through the states of New Jersey, Pennsylvania, West Virginia, Ohio, Indiana, Illinois, Missouri, Colorado, Utah, Nevada, California, and is the border between Nebraska and Kansas. If you live south of this latitude, you'll see a little more of the southern sky and somewhat less of the northern. If you are on the northern side, your view will take in less of the southern sky and more in the other direction.

You will notice that the stars in the charts are not all drawn alike. That is because the stars in the sky are not all the same. They differ in brightness. Stars appear brighter or fainter because of their size, surface temperature and distance from earth. The brightness of a star is known as its magnitude. The brighter the star, the lower the magnitude. The very brightest stars have magnitudes from negative numbers up to about 3. For example, Sirius, the brightest star we can see, has a magnitude of −1.42. The fainter the star, the higher the magnitude. A star with a magnitude of 6 is just barely visible to the naked eye. The charts show the brightest (lowest magnitude) star in each constellation with an asterisk. The second brightest (next lowest magnitude) is represented by a large dot. The other, fainter stars in the constellation are indicated by small dots.

In looking at the stars, you will notice that they also differ in color. A star's color is determined by its surface temperature. The hottest stars are blue in color; they range from about 10,000° K to 60,000° K. Green stars—7,500° K to 10,000° K. White stars—6,000° K to 7,500° K. Yellow stars—5,000° K to 6,000° K. Orange stars—3,500° K to 5,000° K. The coolest are the red stars—3,000° K to 3,500° K.

All stars seem to be twinkling, even though we know that they are giving off a steady light, just like our sun. The twinkling effect is caused by the earth's atmosphere, through which we see the stars. Stars that are low in the sky, just above the horizon, twinkle more because we have to look through more of the dense atmosphere to see them. Stars that are directly overhead flicker less because we are not looking through so much of the dense atmosphere.

The distances to the stars are too vast to be measured like distances here on earth. For this reason, astronomers use a special unit of distance, a light-year. A light-year is the distance that light travels in a year. It is approximately 6 trillion miles. The star Sirius in the constellation Canis Major, for instance, is 8½ light-years away from earth. That means that its light takes 8½ years to reach earth. As stars go, it is the closest star neighbor seen in the Northern Hemisphere. Compare Sirius to the star Deneb in the constellation Cygnus. Deneb is located about 1,500 light-years from earth. The light you see from Deneb left the star 1,500 years ago, soon after the Roman Empire fell in A.D. 476.

Finding Your Direction in the Sky

The star charts will help you know the shapes of the constellations and the brightness of the stars. To find them in the sky, though, you need to know your directions—north, south, east and west.

A good place to start is by finding north, and the simplest and most accurate way to find it is with a compass. Otherwise use a familiar landmark such as a road, building, tree, mountain, lake or similar feature that you know lies north. If none is available, point your left shoulder to the setting sun late in the afternoon. The sun sets in the west. Therefore, you will be facing approximately north. Once you are facing north, your right side is approximately to the east, your back to the south and your left side to the west.

The constellations are also at different heights in the sky. The height can be measured in degrees above the horizon. To get familiar with the measurement of degrees, raise one arm and point straight out to the horizon. That is 0°. Now point straight up directly overhead. That is 90°. Halfway between the horizon and overhead is 45°. One-third the way up is a 30° angle; and two-thirds of the way up is 60°.

Helpful Hints

Plan to stargaze on clear, dark nights. These are nights when there are no clouds in the sky, and it is just before or after a new moon, which casts less light.

If possible, position yourself in a large open space, far from a city or brightly lit buildings. Also try to avoid tall trees and mountains that could block your view of the horizon.

To see the star charts in the book, cover a penlight or small flashlight with a piece of red tissue paper, red cellophane or red cloth. The red light allows you to adjust your vision so that you can see the charts as well as view the stars in the dark sky.

Before starting, give your eyes time to get used to the dark. It may take up to a half hour for your eyes to adapt fully to the dark and allow you to see all the faint stars.

There are two ways you can approach star gazing. One is to look up at the sky and see which bright stars catch your attention. Then open the book to the star chart for that month. Hold the open book over your head. Turn it around so that you can read, straight-side up, the direction you are facing. Then see if you can match the stars you see with the chart in the book.

The other approach is first to read about the best constellations that can be seen on the particular night you are observing. Then hold the star chart overhead, facing in the direction of the constellation. Search the skies in that direction and at the indicated height for the constellation.

A final hint: Remember that the star charts are accurate for the 16th of the month, at 9:00 P.M., as seen from latitude 40° north. If it is earlier in the month, or before 9:00, look for the stars east of where they are shown on the chart. If it is later in the month, or after 9:00, look to the west. If you live south of the 40th parallel, look more to the north. If you live north of that latitude, look toward the south.

Finding the Big Dipper

The best and easiest way to start your star gazing is with the most famous group of stars in the northern sky, the Big Dipper. It is made up of seven bright stars and looks like a cup with a long, bent handle. If you connect four of the stars with an imaginary line you have the cup. If you connect the other three stars you'll find the handle.

The Big Dipper is well-known because it can be seen every clear night, all year long. But you do have to know where to look for it. In the winter months, you can find it to the north and quite low in the sky. Toward spring, look higher and to the northeast. During the summer season, the Big Dipper is still high and in the northwest sky. The fall months see it heading back to the lower part of the northern sky.

As the days of the year pass, the Big Dipper slowly changes its appearance. In the winter, the handle seems to be pointing down. Summertime finds the cup tipping over. The position changes because the earth is constantly moving through its orbit.

The Big Dipper is an asterism, a group of stars that forms a shape in the sky. But it is not a constellation. The Big Dipper is part of a larger group of stars, Ursa Major (the Great Bear), which *is* a constellation.

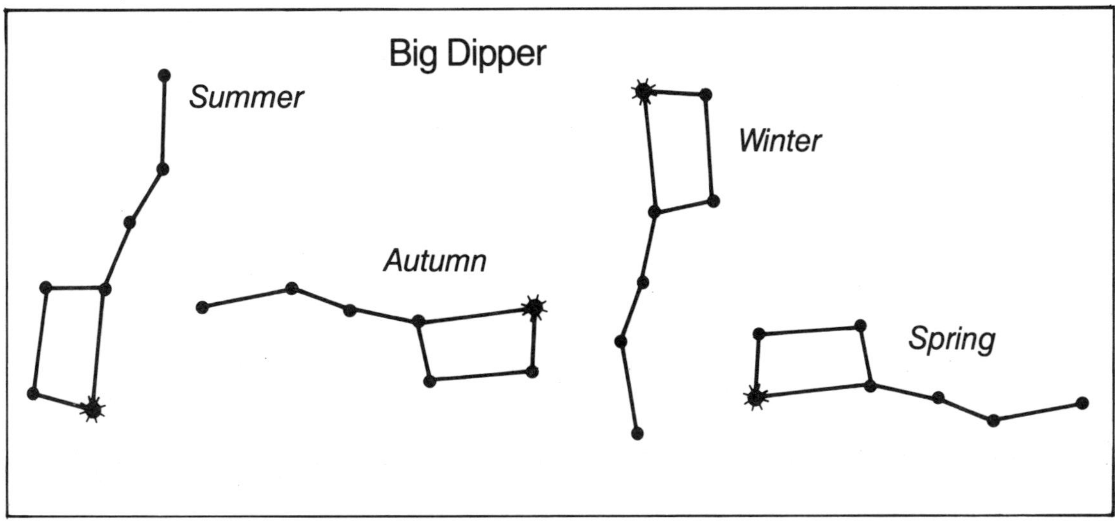

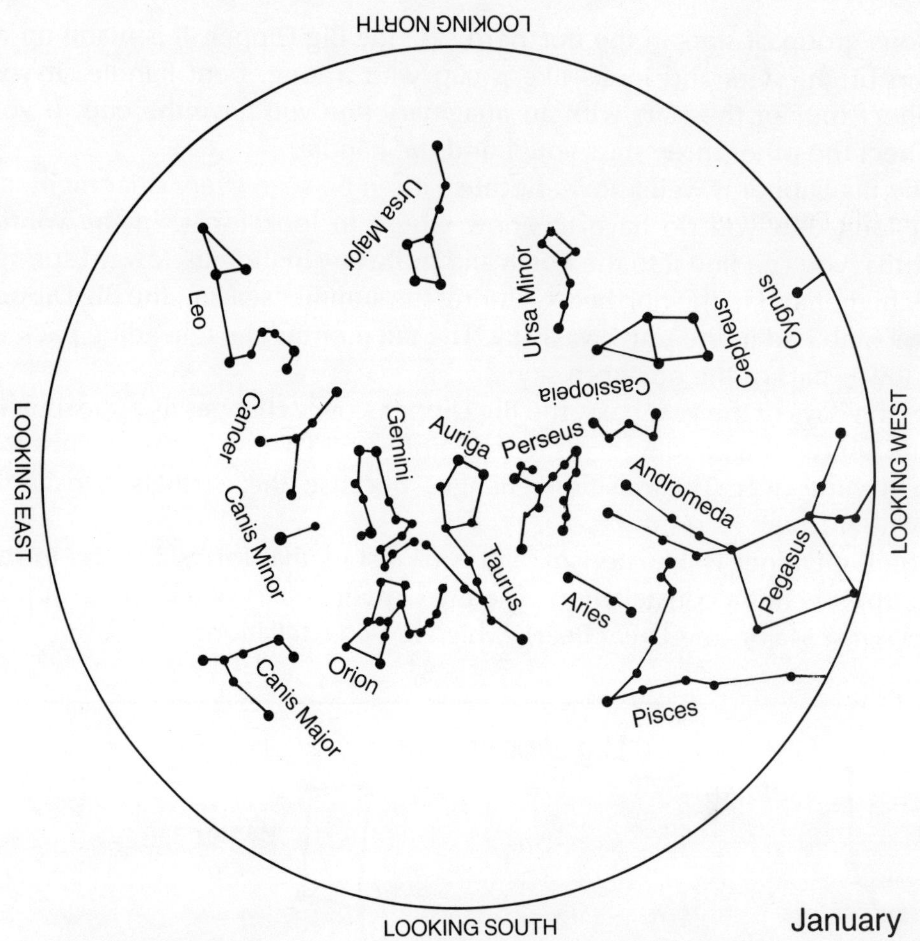

The Stars of January

Few sights are as glorious as a midwinter sky lorded over by the constellation **Orion** (oh-RYE-un), the great Hunter. According to Greek mythology, Orion was put into the heavens by his lover, Artemis, after having been killed by Scorpius, the scorpion.

Orion is probably the easiest constellation to spot. One reason is that it has more bright stars than any other group of stars. To locate Orion, face

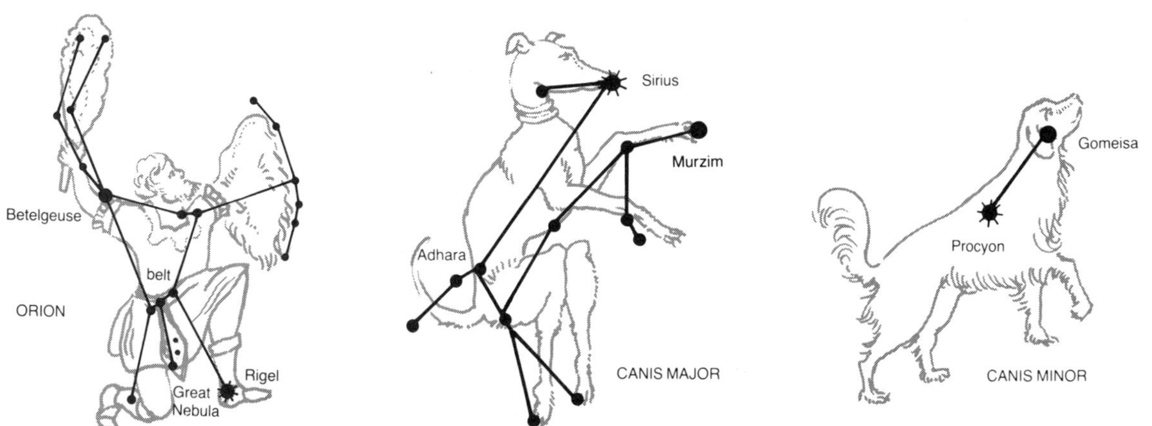

south and turn slightly to the east. Look up at an angle of about 45° from the horizon. The figure looks like a mighty fighter. He holds a raised club in his right hand and a lion-skin shield in his left hand. Hanging from his belt is a huge sword.

The three bright stars in a row, Alnitak, Alnilam and Mintaka, which make up the hunter's belt are the best clue to Orion. The brightest star in the constellation is Rigel (RYE-jell), with a magnitude of 0.1, located 850 light-years from earth. It is at the southwest corner of the constellation, showing the point of Orion's left foot. Betelgeuse (BET-el-jews) is second brightest. Its magnitude is 0.8 and it is 650 light-years away. Betelgeuse is about 400 times as large as our sun. It marks the giant's right shoulder.

What looks like the second faint star on the sword hilt dangling from Orion's belt is not a star at all but a nebula, known as the Great Nebula in Orion. A nebula is a giant cloud of shining gas and dust that looks like a star to the naked eye. Through binoculars or a telescope, though, the Great Nebula appears cloudlike.

Orion, like many other hunters, has well-trained dogs to help him. His two dogs are the constellations **Canis** (KAY-nis) **Major,** the Great Dog, and **Canis Minor,** the Little Dog. As Orion looks off to the west, the two dogs are nearby, to the east and south of him. Canis Major is lower in the sky, about 30° above the horizon. To spot Canis Minor, turn very slightly to the east and look up somewhat higher, to 60°.

Canis Major contains Sirius (SYR-ee-us), the Dog Star, the brightest star in the night sky. Its magnitude is −1.42. The star seems very bright, in part, because it is among the closest of all the stars, only 8½ light-years distant. Since Sirius never rises very high, its rays have to slice through more of the earth's atmosphere than overhead stars. This is why it appears as one of the most twinkly of all stars.

Sirius can be found by tracing an imaginary line southward across the belt stars of Orion. It is the tip of the nose of Canis Major. The left paw is indicated by Murzim, the second brightest star in the constellation. Murzim means "announcer." It got this name because it rises first and is a signal that Sirius is on its way. The third prominent star of Canis Major is Adhara, found on the dog's loin or flank.

The brightest star of the constellation Canis Minor is Procyon (PRO-see-on). It is the eighth brightest star seen from earth, with a magnitude of 0.38. Procyon, which is 11 light-years away, is sometimes called the Little Dog Star. It forms an equilateral triangle with Betelgeuse and Sirius.

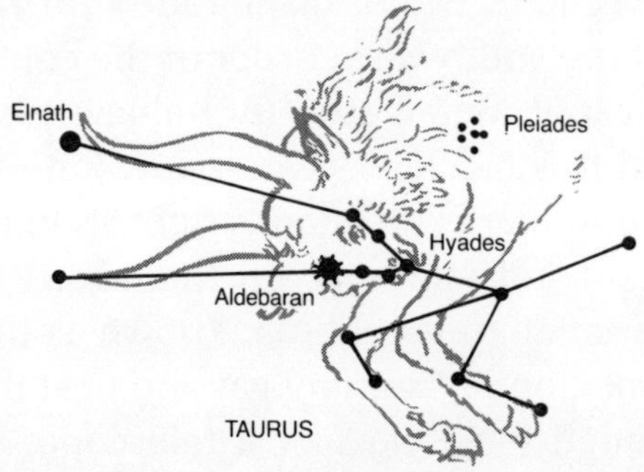

Orion appears to be looking over his left shoulder, past the curved line of stars that make up his shield to the constellation **Taurus** (TAW-rus), the Bull, and seems to be fighting off the bull's attack. To view Taurus, face directly south and look up at an angle of about 60°.

Taurus is a constellation that shows the horns, head, shoulders and forelegs of a mighty bull. It is the second sign of the zodiac. This representation of the bull grew from the Greek legend that held that the animal was really Zeus, king of the gods. The story is that Zeus fell in love with the beautiful maiden Europa. Europa's father, however, did not allow her to see Zeus. Knowing of Europa's fondness for animals, Zeus turned himself into a bull. Europa admired the beast and mounted its back to go for a ride. Zeus immediately swam across the sea to the island of Crete, where he changed back to his own self and married Europa. Since the bull's body was mostly under water during the escape, only its top parts are shown in the constellation.

The brightest star of Taurus, Aldebaran (al-DEB-e-ren), is more than thirty-five times the size of our sun and has a magnitude of 0.9. Aldebaran, which forms the shining right eye of the bull, is 65 light-years distant from earth. The star is in a line with the belt stars of Orion. A nearby V-shaped group of stars, the Hyades (HI-e-deez), outlines the bull's nose. A star cluster called the Pleiades (PLEE-a-deez), or Seven Sisters, forms the shoulder of the bull. In Greek mythology, the Pleiades were the daughters of Atlas who were being pursued by Orion. To save them, Zeus changed them into doves, then into stars.

The Stars of February

The stars of **Auriga** (aw-RYE-gah), the Charioteer, form a five-sided figure, or pentagon, in the sky. You can see Auriga by facing west and looking just beneath the overhead point (the point in the sky directly over your head). Auriga represents the lame son of Minerva and Vulcan. He is holding a goat in

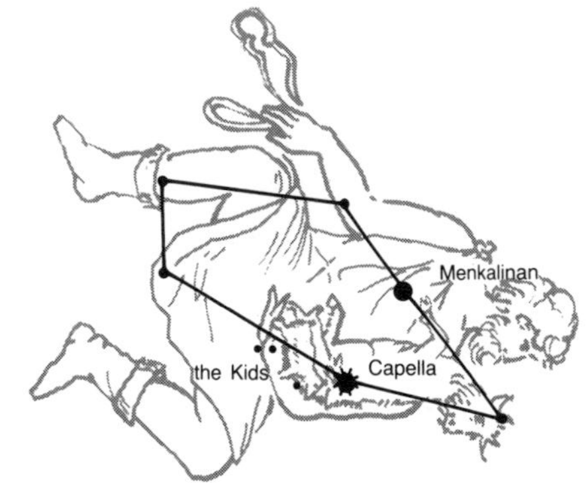

AURIGA

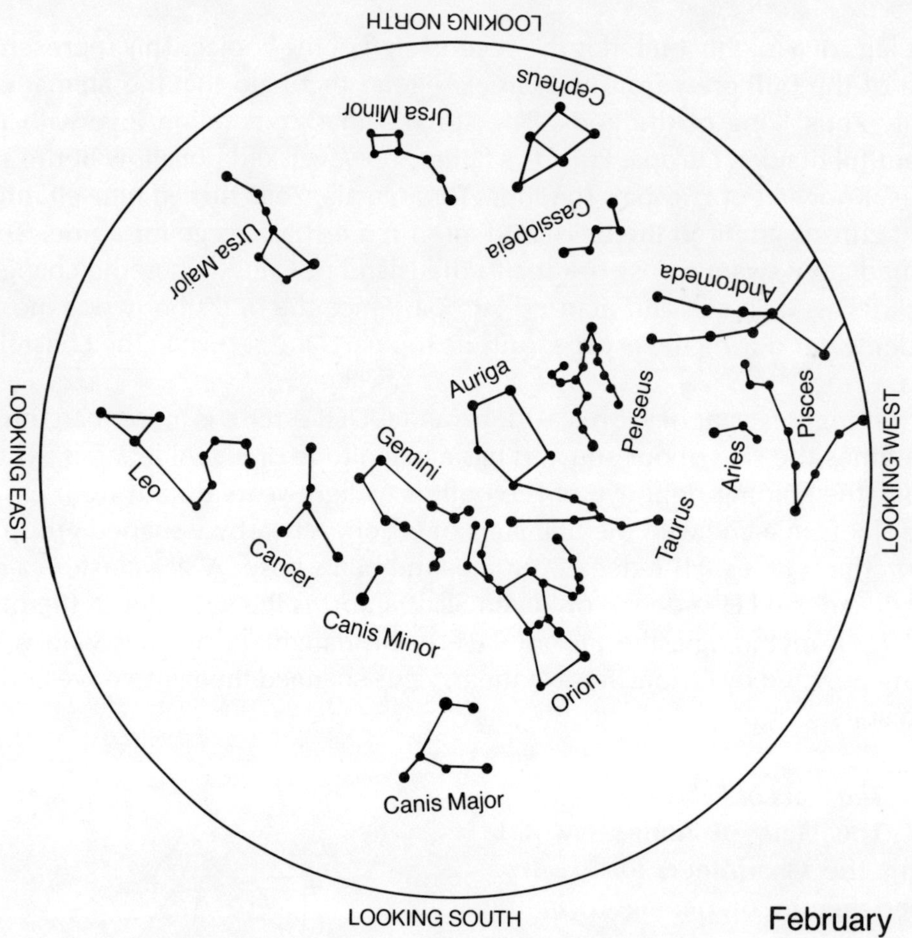

his left arm. In his right hand he grasps a driver's whip. In mythology, Auriga is the god who invented the four-horse chariot to help him get around better. As a reward, Zeus gave him a permanent place in the heavens.

Capella (ke-PEL-eh), the brightest star in Auriga, is the sixth brightest star

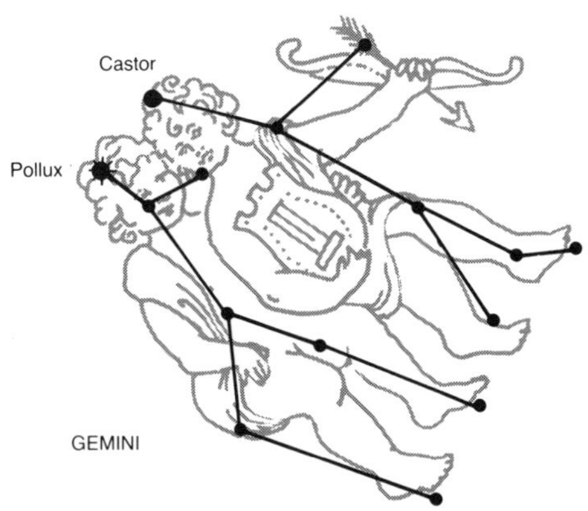

in the sky. It has a magnitude of 0.1, is twelve times the size of our sun and about 45 light-years from earth. The name is Latin for "little she-goat." It is not certain why Auriga is carrying the little goat. Some think it is because the gods trusted only the gentle Auriga to hold the goat whose milk fed Zeus as an infant. Just under Capella is a group of three small stars appropriately named the Kids.

Gemini (JEM-ih-nye), the Twins, is the third sign of the zodiac and a famous group of stars. It is located in the southern sky, between Orion, Canis Minor and the overhead point. The two brightest stars found in the constellation are named for the well-known twins of Greek mythology, Castor (KAS-ter) and Pollux (POL-uks). Pollux is the brighter of the two. It has a magnitude of 1.2, and is 3½ light-years away. The two stars represent the heads of the Twins. The streams of stars below the two bright stars outline their bodies.

One of the earliest legends refers to the stars as the twin pillars that supported King Solomon's temple. Later Greeks named them Pollux, the immortal son of Zeus, and Castor, his mortal brother. When Castor was killed, Pollux begged Zeus to put him to death so he could be united with his brother. Zeus refused, but placed them together in heaven, with a bright star in each one's forehead.

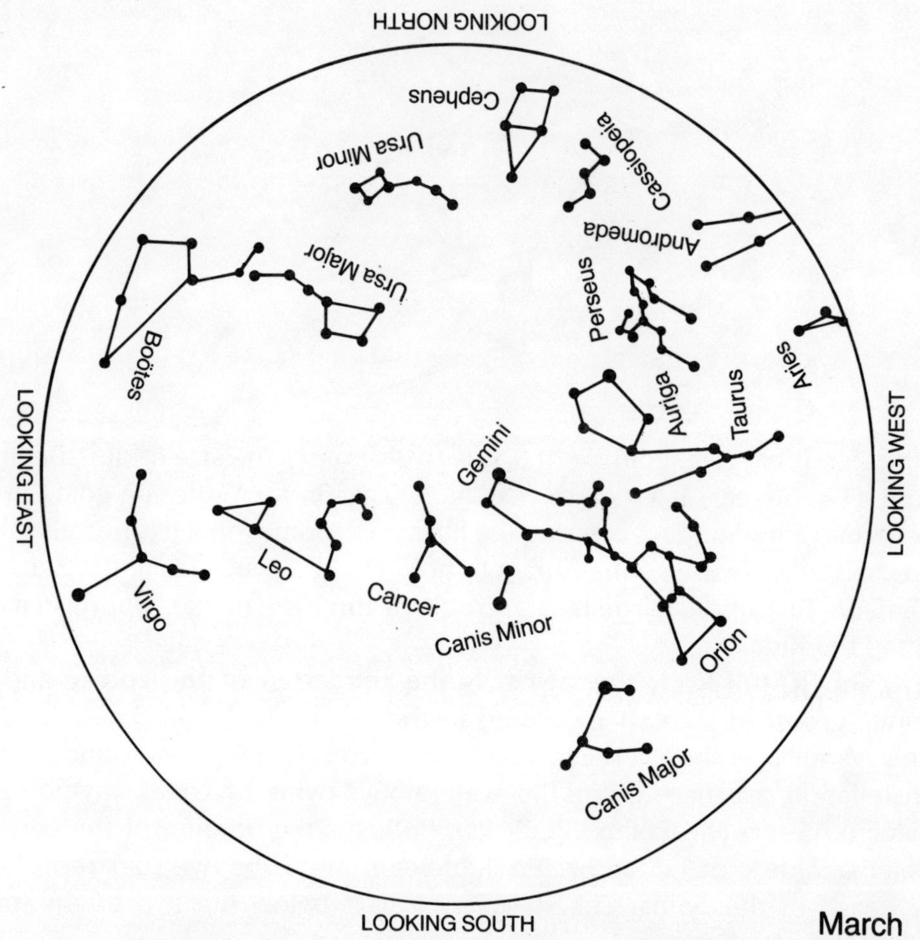

The Stars of March

The single constellation that is at its peak during March is **Cancer,** the Crab. It is found between Gemini and Leo, in the southern sky about 70° above the horizon. Although the well-known fourth sign of the zodiac, Cancer is the least visible constellation. Its brightest star, Acubens (a-CU-

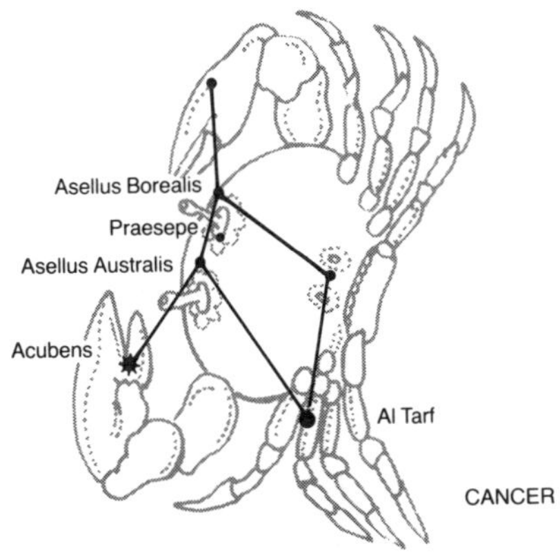

benz), from the Arabic *Al Zubenack* ("the claws"), marks the Crab's southern claw.

Cancer was sent by Hera, wife of Zeus, to punish Hercules in battle. When Hercules succeeded in crushing Cancer, Hera awarded the fallen hero a place of honor among the stars.

Two faint stars, Asellus Borealis (a-SELL-us-bohr-ee-AL-is), the Northern Ass, and Asellus Australis (a-SELL-us-awe-STRAL-is), the Southern Ass, in the constellation Cancer are sometimes visible to the naked eye on a clear night. They are said to have frightened off the enemies of the Greek gods by braying very loudly. In gratitude the gods set them in the sky with a star representing a manger between them. Praesepe (pree-SEE-pee) is actually not one star, but a cluster of nearly 400 stars, sometimes called the Beehive.

The Stars of April

Leo, the Lion, the fifth sign of the zodiac, is the most splendid of the spring constellations. It stretches across the southern sky at about 70° above the horizon.

Legend has it that the majestic Nemean Lion was the most powerful beast in ancient times. It was believed to have been so strong that no weapon could pierce its skin. The only way Hercules could slay Leo (as one of his twelve labors) was by trapping it in a cave and strangling it with his bare hands. Hera, the wife of Zeus, raised the soul of the brave lion into a constellation of stars in the heavens.

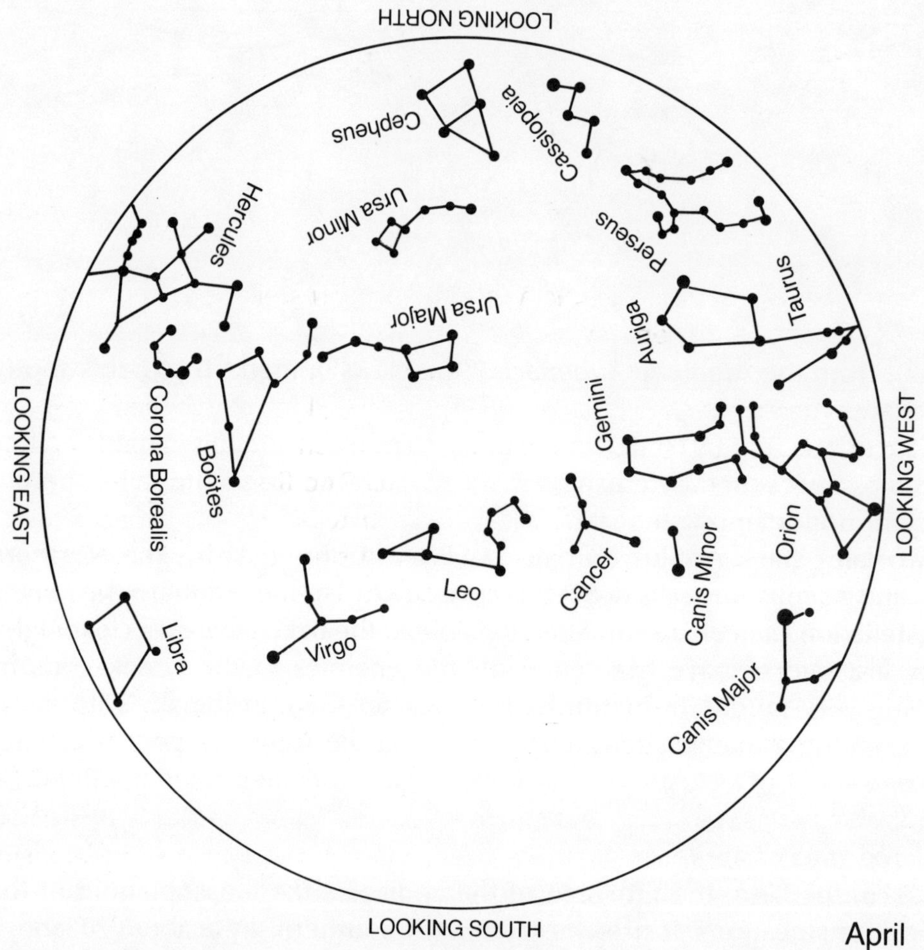

April

The brightest star in Leo is Regulus (REG-you-lus), the Prince. It is about 55 light-years away from us, and has a magnitude of 1.36. Regulus is the star at the handle of a sickle, or the dot of a backward question mark, that forms the front of the lion, from the top of its nose, along its mane to its two front paws. The lion's tail is marked by the second brightest star in the constellation, Denebola (de-NEB-oh-la), magnitude 2.23.

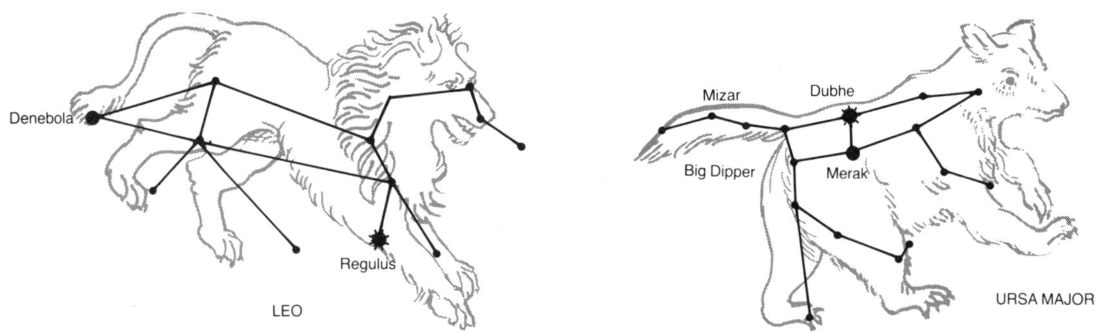

Ursa Major, the Great Bear, is another April constellation. You will recall that it is the constellation that includes the Big Dipper. The handle of the Big Dipper outlines the bear's tail, the cup marks its hindquarters. Ursa Major is in the northern sky, slightly to the east, and about 60° above the horizon.

The two stars in the front of the cup are often called the pointer stars because they point to Polaris, the North Star. The first is Dubhe (DUB-ee), the brightest star (magnitude 1.95) in the constellation; the other is Merak (MEE-rack), the Great Bear's second brightest star (magnitude 2.37). If you follow an imaginary line north from Merak to Dubhe, and continue about five times its length, you arrive at Polaris near the center of the night sky.

The other stars of Ursa Major are not very bright. Of special interest, though, is Mizar (MY-zar), the star found in the crook of the handle. It has a twin, Alcor (AL-cor). Although they almost appear to be one star, Alcor and Mizar are actually far apart in space. People in England refer to the pair as "Jack and His Wagon." In ancient Arabia, they were used as a test of the eyesight of archers in the Sultan's army. Only those with very keen vision could make out that there were two separate stars.

According to Greek mythology, Zeus fell in love with Callisto (Ke-LIS-toe), a beautiful nymph. When Hera learned that her husband was being unfaithful, she changed Callisto into a bear. Later, Callisto's son, Arias, came across the bear in the forest. Not knowing it was his mother, he tried to shoot it with an arrow. Zeus saw this and immediately changed Arias into a bear, too. He then set both bears into the sky. Callisto became Ursa Major; Arias became Ursa Minor, the Little Bear. Because Zeus tugged so hard on their tails to raise them to the sky, these two bears have unusually long tails.

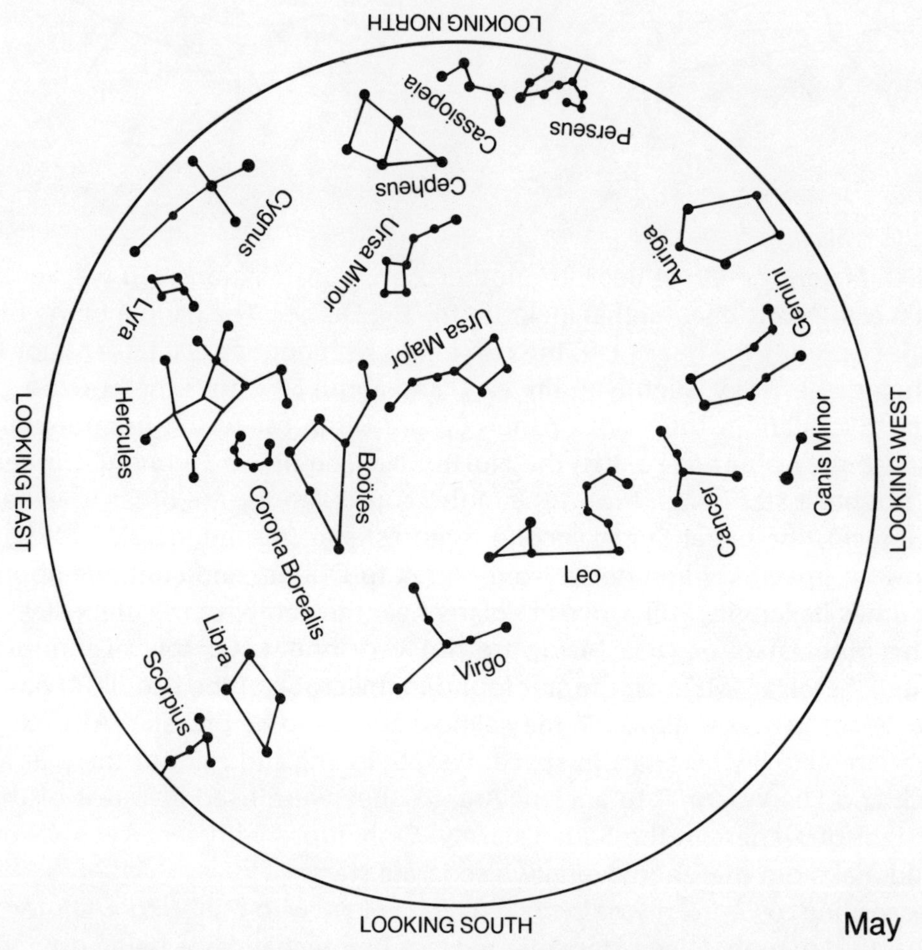

The Stars of May

The stars of the constellation **Virgo** (VER-go), from the Latin meaning "virgin," form an irregular shape in the sky. They make up the sixth sign of the zodiac. Look for Virgo directly south and 45° above the horizon.

The most usual representation of this constellation shows a reclining

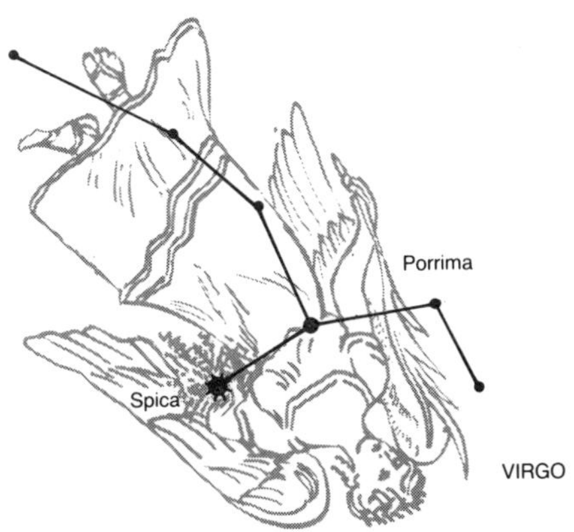

woman. In the figure's left hand is the flower of a wheat plant marked by the star Spica (SPY-kah), Latin for "ear of wheat." Spica, the brightest star in Virgo, gives off as much light as 2,440 suns. It is located 260 light-years from earth and has a magnitude of 1.

The legend of the constellation Virgo comes from a myth told by different peoples about the coming of spring. The earth goddess Virgo has been traced back to very early times when different people worshiped some maiden whom they associated with the harvest. In Egypt she was called Isis; the Hebrews named her Bethulah; Persians worshiped Khosha; the Greeks, Ceres; and the Romans, Demeter. In the legend of Isis, for example, we are told that Isis once accidentally shook a sheaf of wheat, scattering the grains and thereby creating the Milky Way.

The Stars of June

The constellation **Boötes** (boh-OH-teez), often called the Herdsman, is easy to locate; it is about 90° above the horizon in the southern sky. Its leading star, Arcturus (arc-TEW-russ), the fourth brightest star in the sky, has a magnitide of −0.1. This star is about thirty times the size of the sun, but it is 36 light-years away. Arcturus is well-known for its bright orange color. The Greeks named the star Arcturus, meaning "bear keeper," because it seems to follow the bear constellations Ursa Major and Ursa Minor across the sky. To find Arcturus, trace the path of the three stars in the handle of the Big Dipper out to the brightest star you can see in the area.

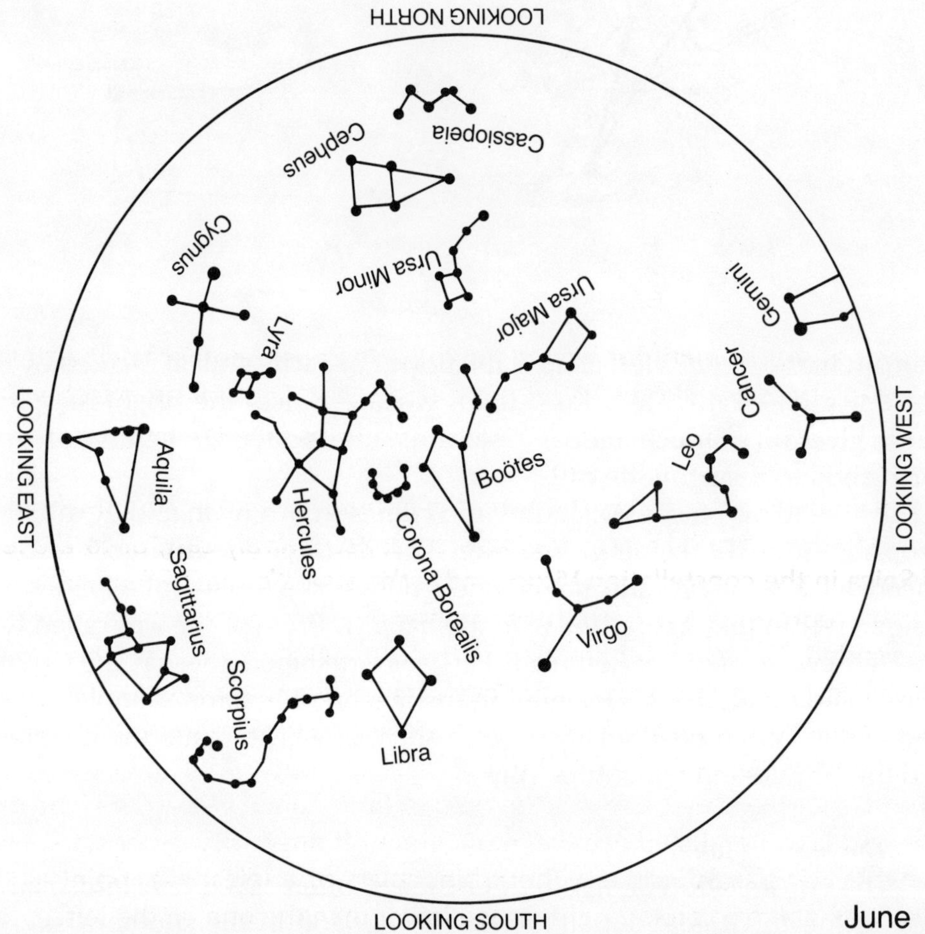

Boötes is a kite-like figure that is usually pictured as a hunter with a staff in his right hand. Arcturus is at the hem of his robe. The other bright stars in Boötes are Micar (MY-car), on his staff, and Nakkar (NAK-kar), on the edge of his robe.

Mythology has many explanations for the presence of Boötes in the sky. According to one legend, Boötes was condemned to hold up the heavens

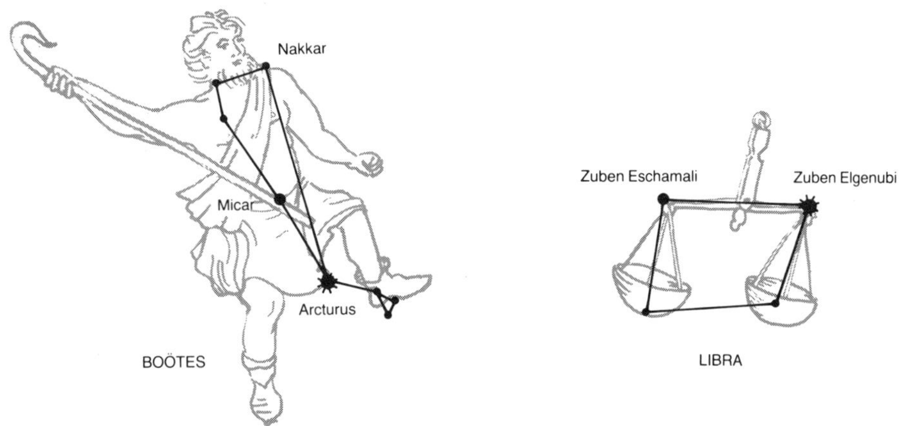

forever as punishment for having fought with Zeus. Another tale has it that the gods ordered Boötes to follow Callisto, the Great Bear, and her son Arias, the Little Bear, keeping them in their orbits. This explains the staff, or bear-prod, he holds in his hand.

Low in the southern sky, at a height of about 30°, you can find the boxlike constellation **Libra** (LEE-bra), the Balance. It lies entirely east, or to the left, of Spica in the constellation Virgo, and is the seventh sign of the zodiac.

Libra represents a balance beam from which a pair of weighing scales is suspended. The two brightest stars in the constellation, Zuben Elgenubi (the Southern Claw) to the west and Zuben Eschamali (the Northern Claw) to the east, outline the beam. The tongue-twisting names originated in ancient Greece when Libra was part of the constellation Scorpius. They are rather faint to the naked eye, and may be hard to find. Zuben Eschamali is the only star visible to the naked eye that has a greenish tinge. Two other stars, even dimmer and barely visible without binoculars or a telescope, point to the two pans, the one on the right tipped lower than the one on the left.

Libra is one of the few constellations that does not deal with a living creature of some sort; it is the only object in the zodiac. To the Egyptians, Libra symbolized the scales of justice on which the human heart would be weighed after death. Other ancient people used it to represent the scale on which all human deeds are measured. The Chinese put the constellation's appearance to a practical purpose: At the time each year when the constella-

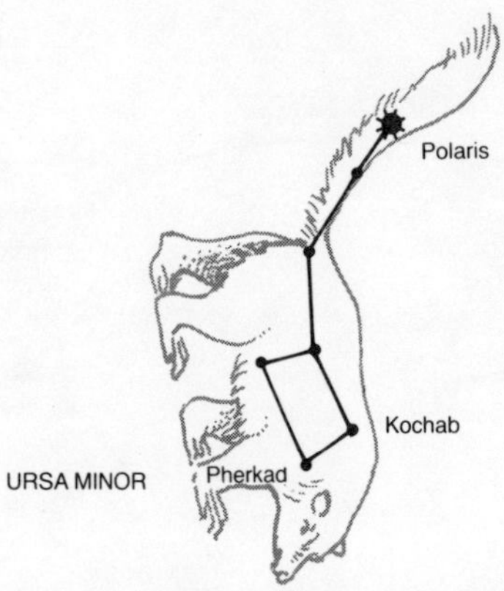

tion became most clearly visible, the country's weights were checked for accuracy according to Chinese law. It is interesting to note that in the Northern Hemisphere, the constellation is most visible in June when the hours of light and dark are the same, or balanced.

June is also the best time to see **Ursa Minor,** the Little Bear. This constellation can be found by looking north at an angle slightly above 30°. Just as Ursa Major contains the Big Dipper, Ursa Minor is outlined by a similar seven-star pattern, the Little Dipper. The body of the Little Bear is made up of the four stars in the cup; its tail consists of the three stars of the handle.

Ursa Minor is best found by locating the two pointer stars of the Big Dipper, Merak and Dubhe, in the constellation Ursa Major. Continue a line from Merak through Dubhe for about five times the distance between them. This will bring you to Polaris, a fairly bright star at the end of the handle of the Little Dipper. Polaris is the brightest star in the constellation. It is both the end of the Little Dipper handle and the tip of the Little Bear's tail.

Polaris is also called Polestar or, more commonly, the North Star. Located near the North Pole, it barely moves at all throughout the year, in contrast to the other stars. For this reason it is the star that has long guided sailors and navigators.

Besides Polaris, the two other bright stars of Ursa Minor are Kochab (KO-kab) and Pherkad (FER-kad), often called the Guardian Stars. They are located on the side of the cup away from the handle.

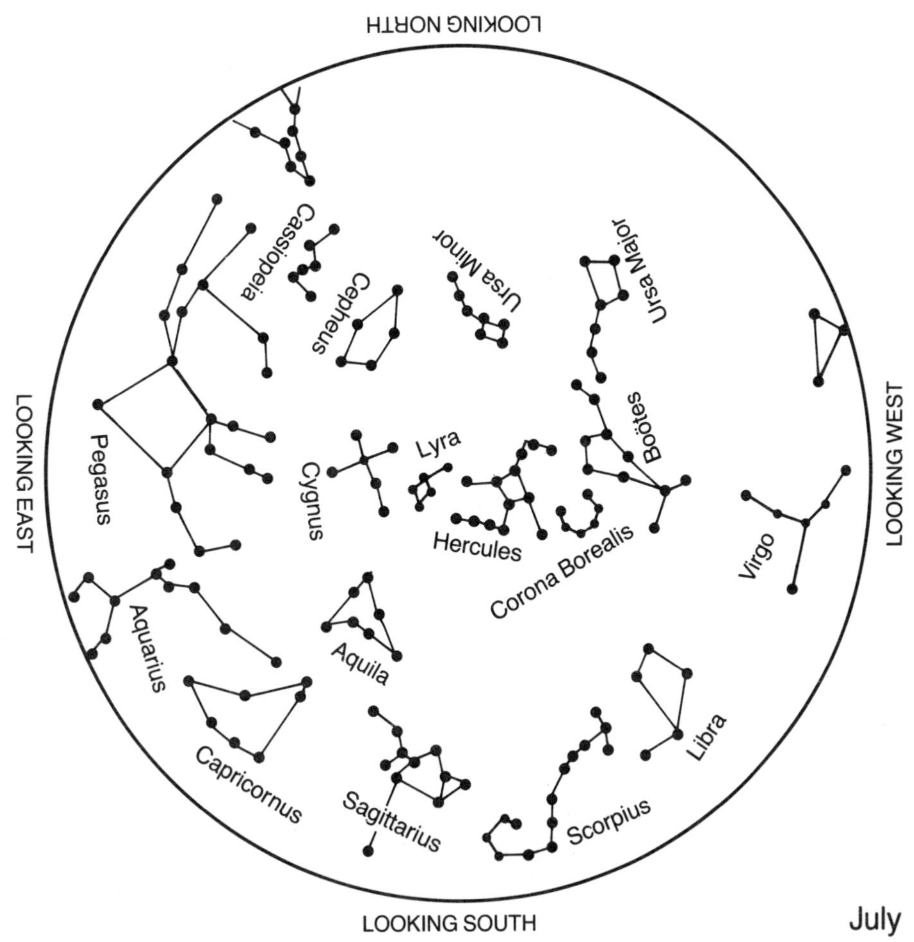

The Stars of July

The **Corona Borealis** (koh-ROH-nuh-bohr-ee-AL-is), Latin for "northern crown," is a beautiful small constellation located to the left, or east, of Boötes. To sight it, turn slightly to your right as you face south, and look just short of directly overhead.

The seven stars that make up the Corona Borealis form a semicircle, which is seen as the outline of a shining crown in the sky. Alphecca (al-FECK-a) is the brightest star of this constellation. Nusakan (new-SOCK-en) is the second brightest. The other stars appear very faint to the naked eye.

The ancient Greeks, enthralled by the beauty of the Corona Borealis, told the story of Princess Ariadne of Crete who fell in love with Theseus. One day Theseus sailed away and failed to return to Ariadne. The god Bacchus saw her weeping and fell in love with her. He asked her to marry him and gave her his most beautiful gold and jeweled crown to wear. When she died at an early age, Bacchus set the crown of seven shining stars in the sky to honor her.

To the east of the Corona Borealis and extending eastward from the overhead point is the constellation **Hercules** (HER-cu-lees), the Strong Man. This popular and very powerful hero of Greek mythology is pictured as a kneeling giant, usually upside down to the observer.

All of the twenty or so stars of the constellation Hercules are quite dim to the naked eye. Kornephoros (kor-NEF-o-russ), at the giant's right shoulder, is one of the largest stars. Another massive star, Ras Algethi (ras-al-JEE-thee), Arabic for "kneeler's head," is a red star that marks the head of Hercules. It lies toward the south and is said to be 6,000 times the size of the sun.

Hercules' midsection forms a geometric shape that is known as the Keystone. On the side of the Keystone that lies near the Corona Borealis there is a faint glow in the sky. This is a globular cluster of about 50,000 or

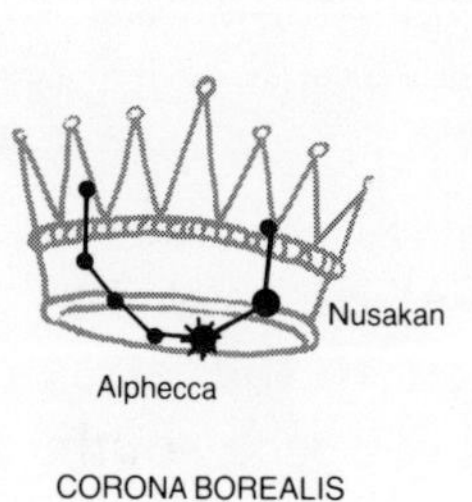

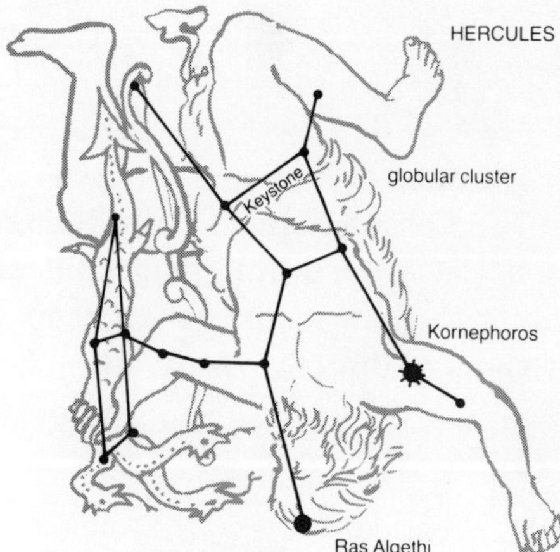

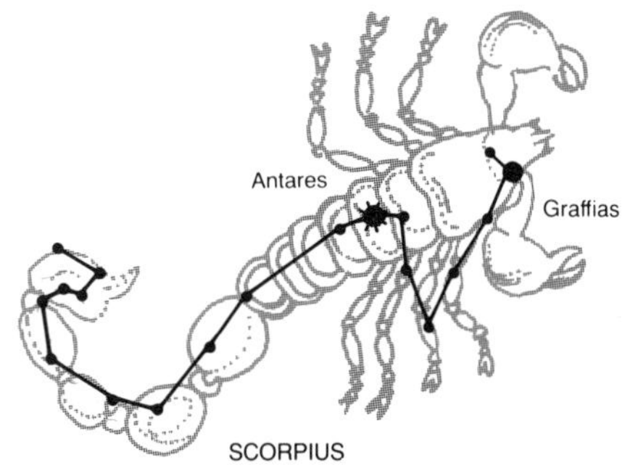

more stars, all crowded so tightly together that it is impossible to get an accurate count. Under good conditions, the cluster can help you spot Hercules. It is staggering to realize that this cluster is more than 30,000 light-years from earth!

The constellation **Scorpius** (SCOR-pee-us), or the Scorpion, appears directly south and barely above the horizon during the summer. It is the eighth sign of the zodiac. The head of Scorpius faces west; at the southeastern end is its tail and stinger. Scorpius is so low in the sky that its stars always appear to be twinkling. If you live in a northern part of the United States you will be able to see only the top of its body.

The brightest star of Scorpius is Antares (an-TAIR-eez), with a magnitude of 1.1. It is 430 light-years away. Antares shines with a bright red light that can be seen with the unaided eye. Found toward the upper part of Scorpius, Antares is sometimes considered the heart of the Scorpion.

As the Greeks tell it, Scorpius became a constellation because of Orion's boast that he could kill every animal on earth. The fearful gods sent a giant scorpion to kill Orion, and when the scorpion succeeded, the gods rewarded him with a place in the sky, but far from Orion. The fact is, the two constellations are never in the sky at the same time.

The Stars of August

Lyra (LYE-ra), the Lyre, is a small constellation that contains the brilliant 0 magnitude Vega, the fifth brightest star seen from earth. Twenty-six light-

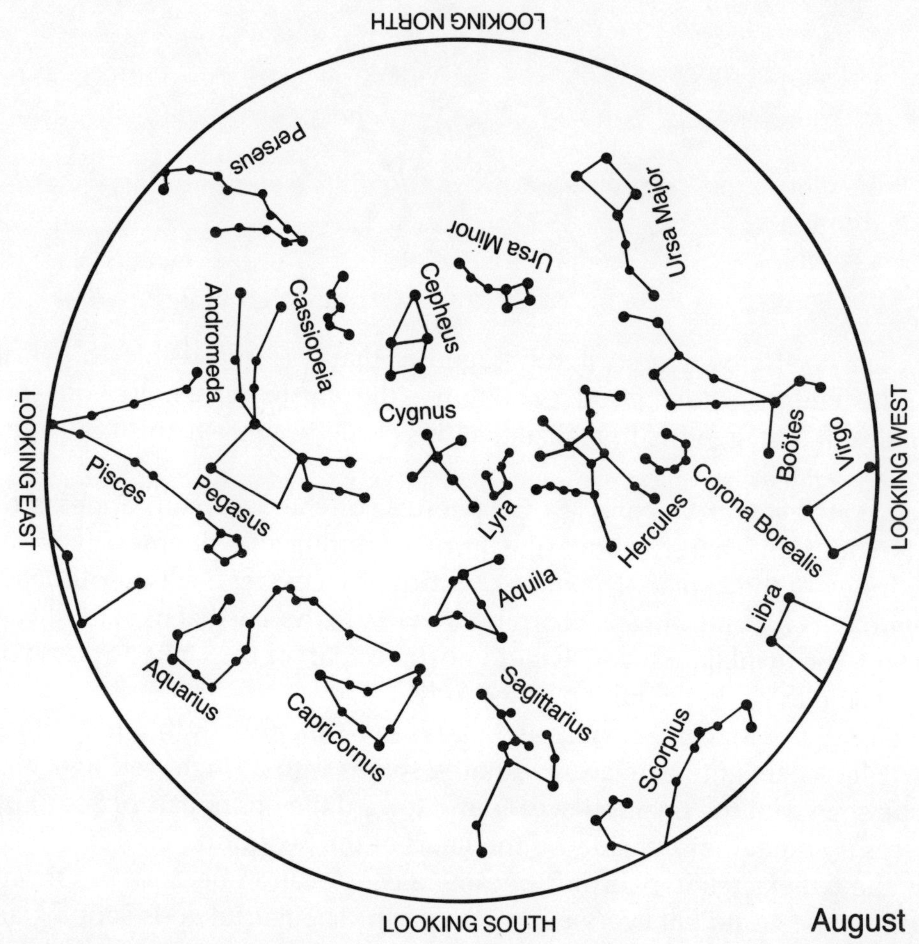

years distant, Vega is visible to the eyes as a pale blue star. Because of Vega, the constellation Lyra dominates the summer sky. It is found in the south nearly directly overhead, and just to the east of Hercules.

The lyre, a harplike musical instrument, was a favorite of the ancient Greeks. In a Greek myth, Orpheus played sad melodies on his lyre, mourning his dead wife, Euridice. Pluto, the god of the lower world, finally agreed to let Orpheus bring Euridice back, provided that Orpheus not look at her until she was above ground. Unfortunately, Orpheus couldn't resist turning around to see if she was following him, and so he lost Euridice forever. After Orpheus died, Zeus remembered his soulful music and raised the lyre to a place among the other stars.

In addition to the very bright Vega at the top of one of Lyra's arms, the constellation has five other notable stars. All are quite faint, however. The one to the east of Vega is visible on a clear, dark night as a pair of stars, one right next to the other. Through a telescope, however, you will find that each of these stars is a double. That is, it has a close-by partner, which makes a total of four stars! The other four stars form a parallelogram, north-south in its long direction. The sides of the parallelogram outline the lyre's strings.

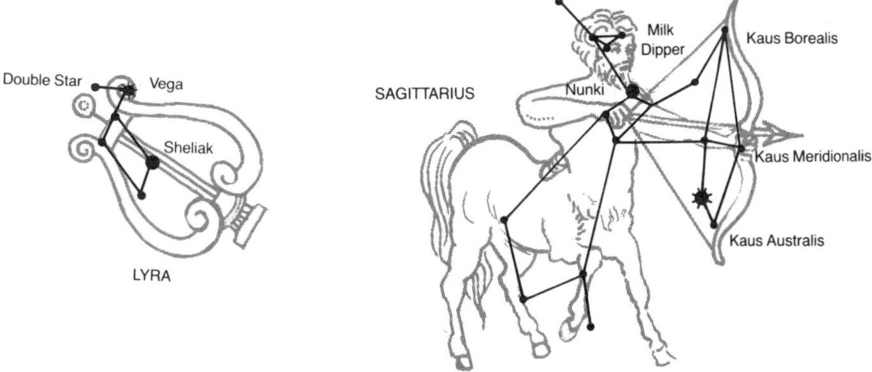

Sagittarius (saj-ih-TAIR-ee-us), the Archer, is a group of stars found directly to the south, and low in the sky, about 30° above the horizon. It is the ninth sign of the zodiac. Sagittarius has no very bright stars and its shape can be hard to detect, but it is certainly worth the effort. In Sagittarius you are looking at the Milky Way. That is the very heart of our galaxy, a great star cloud of some 100 billion stars.

To the Greeks, the arc of three stars facing west brought an image of a bow to mind. The remaining six or so stars in the constellation suggested a centaur, with the upper part a man's body and the lower part a horse. They wove the following legend around the pattern of stars: Chiron, a mythical centaur, was very wise and trained many Greek heroes to excel in archery. Chiron was accidentally shot by one of Hercules' poisoned arrows, but because Chiron was immortal, he did not die. He suffered greatly, however. So he begged Zeus, king of the gods, to allow him to die as a mortal. Zeus took pity on Chiron, and not only granted his wish, but assigned him a place among the stars.

Other stargazers, noticing the arc of three stars within the constellation conjured up another image. They saw a small upside-down dipper which they called the Milk Dipper. The handle points northwest (the top of Sagittarius' bow); the bowl is outlined with stars. They called the small dipper the Milk dipper because Sagittarius is in the middle of the richest part of the broad band of stars that we call the Milky Way.

Some modern observers have hit on still another way to locate Sagittarius. They see the outline of a teapot tilted in the direction of Scorpius' tail. Perhaps you too will find it easier to find the teapot shape than the centaur or the Milk Dipper.

The brightest star in Sagittarius is Kaus Australis (kows-aus-TRAL-is), southern bow, which has a magnitude of 1.8. It appears at the bottom of the bow. Marking the rest of the bow are Kaus Meridionalis, middle bow, and Kaus Borealis, northern bow. Nunki, the second brightest star in the constellation (magnitude 2.1), forms the shoulder of the archer's left arm holding the bow.

Almost every one of the ancient civilizations saw in the constellation **Aquila** (ACK-will-a), the Eagle, a huge and powerful bird flying toward the east. Aquila is found in the southern sky just above Sagittarius, about 60° over the horizon.

The head of the mighty eagle is defined by three stars. Most prominent is the very bright star at the center called Altair (al-TAIR), with a magnitude of

0.8. It is also one of our closest star neighbors, only 16 light-years away. It gives off about ten times as much light as the sun. North of Altair is the second brightest star, Tarazed (TAHR-a-zed); just south is Alshain (al-SHAIN). The rest of the stars in the constellation outline the eagle's body and immense wing spread.

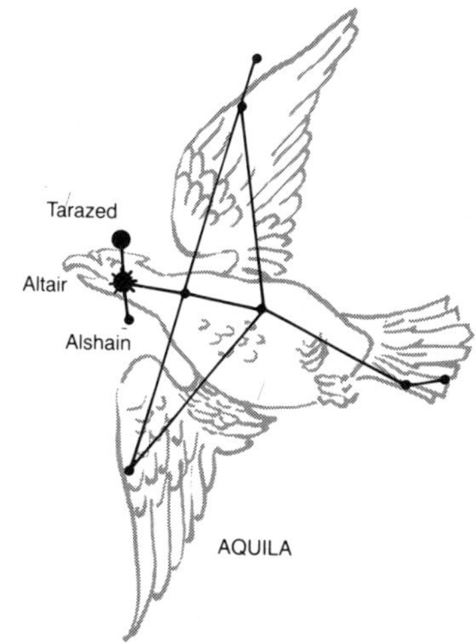

The Greek myths tell us that a splendid eagle named Aquila waited on Zeus to do his bidding. One time Zeus asked Aquila to fly down to earth and find the most beautiful youth, who would become cup-bearer to the gods and bring them their nectar. The eagle swooped down and after a long search chose the youth Ganymede. The eagle lifted the handsome lad and brought him up to Zeus. Zeus was so happy with Aquila's choice that he rewarded the eagle with a permanent place in the sky.

The Stars of September

Cygnus (SIG-nus), the Swan, is found slightly north of Lyra, near the overhead point when facing west. A rather bright star, Deneb (DEN-eb), magnitude 1.3, but 1,500 light-years away, marks the tail of the constellation. Deneb is one of the three bright stars that make up the so-called Summer Triangle. The others are Altair (in Aquila), to the south, and Vega (in Lyra), to the west.

The constellation Cygnus is usually pictured as a flying swan with short tail, wide wingspan and long neck, heading to the southwest. The second brightest star, Albireo (al-BEER-ee-oh), is at the swan's head. With binoculars or a telescope Albireo can be seen as one of a pair of stars.

Greek legend relates how Phaeton borrowed the chariot of the sun god one day. He drove it so dangerously close to earth that Zeus struck him down with a bolt of lightning to save the world from destruction. The wildly

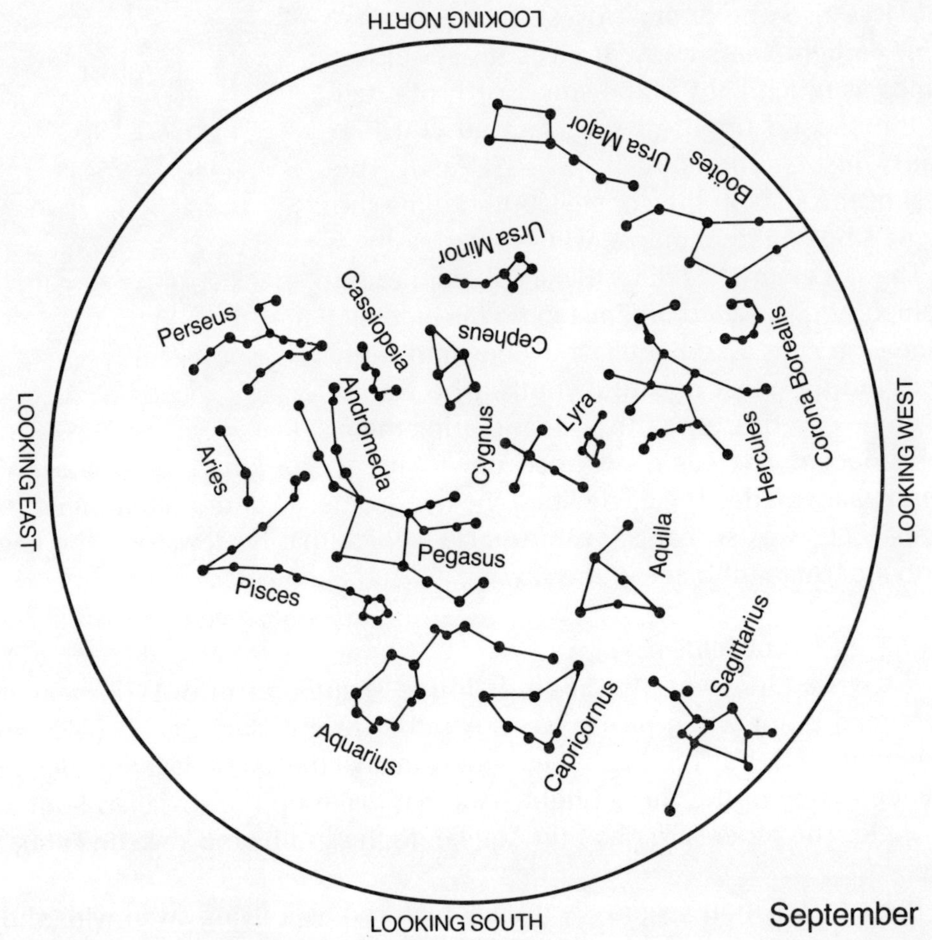

September

speeding chariot crashed into the river Eridanus, killing Phaeton. Cygnus, Phaeton's devoted friend, dove into the river again and again in a vain attempt to try to recover the body. The gods thought Cygnus looked so much like a swan diving for food that they took pity on him and transformed him into a swan in the sky.

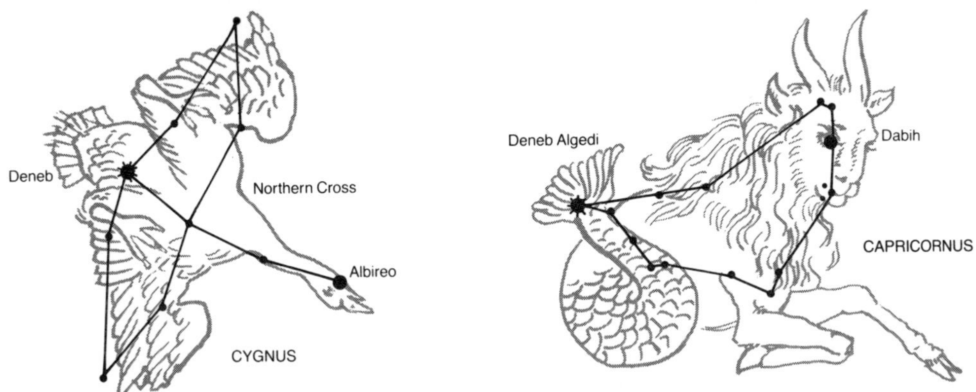

To the early Christians, the constellation resembled a cross, the so-called Northern Cross, rather than a swan. A straight line of stars runs from Deneb at its tip down toward the horizon in the southwest. Another row of stars intersects this line to form the cross.

Cygnus lies in the midst of the Milky Way. On a clear night you can see a dark patch blotting out part of the Milky Way near Deneb. Astronomers call this the Northern Coal Sack; it is actually an immense cloud of stellar dust that does not allow the light of the stars behind it to pass through.

Capricornus (cap-ri-CORN-us), the Sea Goat, is difficult to locate because it contains no bright stars and little clear form. Ancients gave it the name Sea Goat because they pictured it as a creature with a goat's head and the tail of a fish. Look for Capricornus in a southerly direction, about 30° up from the horizon. It is the tenth sign of the zodiac.

The brightest star in Capricornus is Deneb Algedi (DEN-eb-al-JEE-dee), a yellow double star that is near the end of the animal's tail. In the head of the goat is a pair of double stars called Dabih (DAY-bee) Major and Dabih Minor. The outlined figure of Capricornus somewhat resembles a large V-shape, bent on its side.

One legend represents Capricornus as a transformation of the Greek god Pan, who was half goat and half man. One time, the story goes, the monster Typhon was pursuing Pan. In his great fright, Pan plunged into the Nile to escape. He saved himself from drowning by changing the lower part of his body into a fishtail. The rest remained goatlike. In his new form the gods raised him to a place in the sky as the constellation Capricornus.

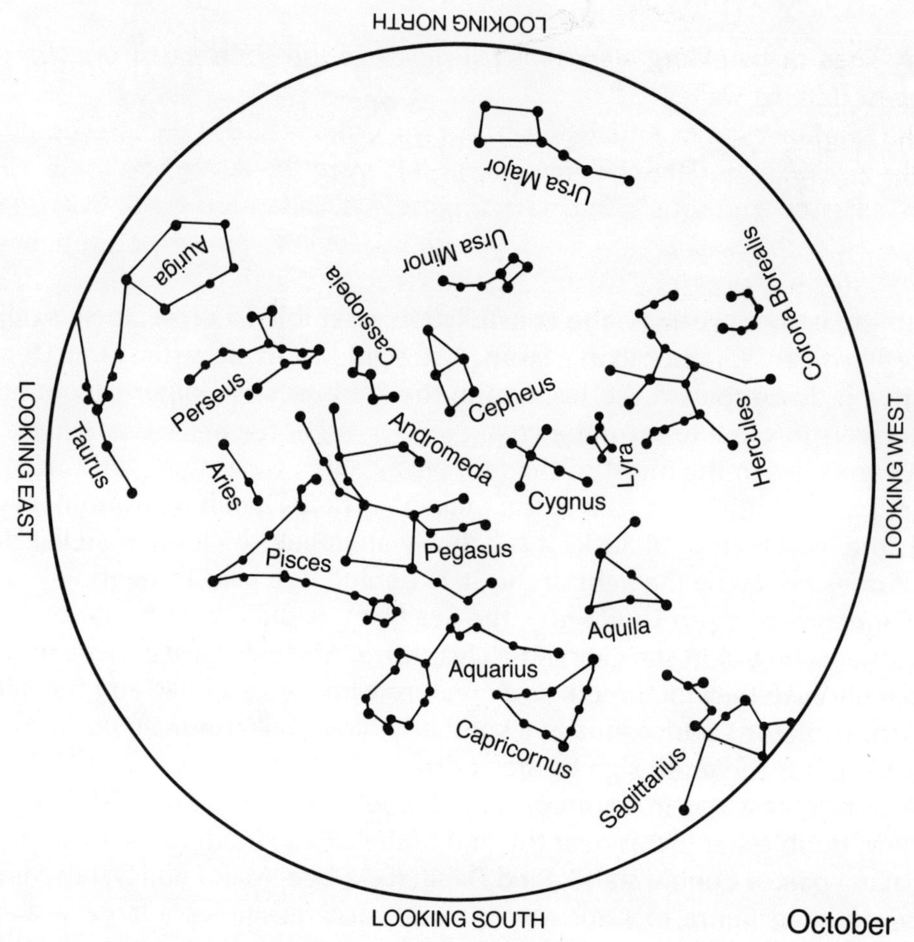

October

The Stars of October

About 45° above the horizon facing south lies **Aquarius** (uh-KWAIR-ih-us), the Water Carrier, the eleventh constellation in the zodiac. Aquarius is a faint and rather formless constellation. It depicts a man pouring water out of a jug, which is made up of four stars in a Y-shape. To the naked eye, the dim, wavy lines of twinkling stars that fall down to the southeast from the jug suggest flowing water.

The brightest star in Aquarius, west of the Y-shape and at the left shoulder of the figure, is Sadalmelik (sad'l-MELL-ik), from the Arabic meaning "the Lucky Star of the King." The next brightest is Sadalsuud (sad'l-SUE-udd), "Luckiest of the Lucky." It is in a line with Sadalmelik, but to the southwest.

Aquarius is an ancient symbol that is associated with running water. The Egyptians believed that Aquarius caused the river Nile to overflow its banks, bringing water to the nearby farmlands. And in Greek myths, the Water Carrier is the giver of life. To people in lands where water was scarce, Aquarius was considered a kindly god who brought the necessary rains.

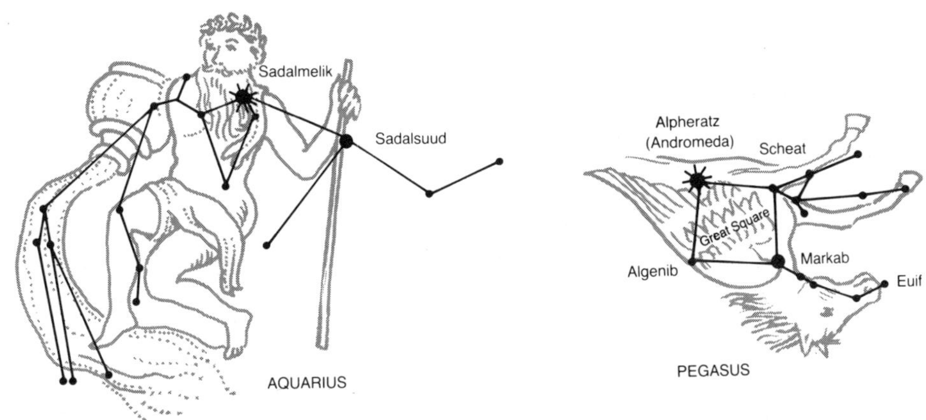

The constellation **Pegasus** (PEG-uh-sus), the Flying Horse, is formed around a giant square called the Great Square of Pegasus, with four nearly equally bright stars at the corners. The constellation is found high up in the southeast sky, at an altitude of about 70°. Within the Great Square can be spotted any number of faint stars. How many can you see? The record naked-eye sighting is 102, though an average observer may pick out up to 30.

The name Pegasus comes from the winged flying horse in Greek mythology who was born from the head of Medusa. Bellerophon rode Pegasus when he conquered the fire-breathing monster Chimera. The young hero became too proud, though, so Pegasus threw him off and flew up to the stars to find a place in the heavens.

The constellation is always seen upside down, with the stars marking only the forequarters, head and wings of Pegasus. The bright star Alpheratz (al-FEE-ratz) is in the upper lefthand corner of the Great Square. In Pegasus, the star points to the middle of the creature's belly. In the nearby constellation of Andromeda (an-DROM-e-da), the same star forms Andromeda's head. Markab (MAR-kab), Arabic for "saddle," is the bottom right star in the Great Square.

The Stars of November

Pisces (PI-seez), the Fishes, is a large V-shaped constellation, and the twelfth sign of the zodiac. The arms of the V-shape open toward the northwest and the Great Square of Pegasus. The bottom of the V is about 60° above the horizon and can be found in the southern sky, slightly to the east. Although Pisces contains no very bright stars, it is an important constellation because the sun passes through it during the vernal equinox, the first day of spring.

Pisces was given its name because it was thought to show a pair of fishes, the Northern Fish and the Western Fish, hanging at the ends of two long knotted fish lines. The brightest star in the constellation, Al Rischa (al-RISH-a), which comes from the Arabic word for "cord," is at the knot in the lines.

To find the Western Fish, follow the "fish line" of stars to the west and you will arrive at the Circlet, a five-star pentagon lying right under the Great

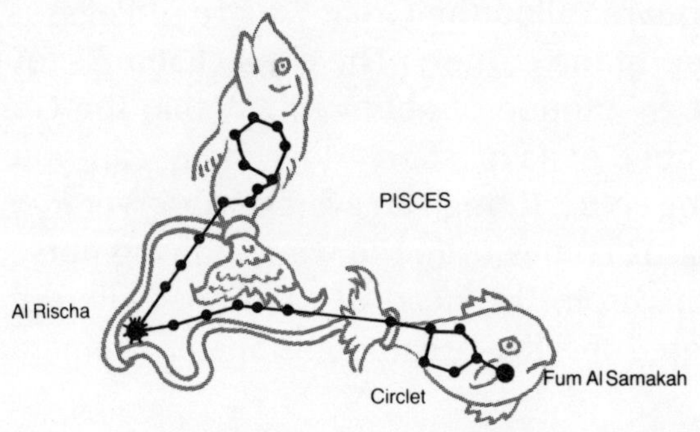

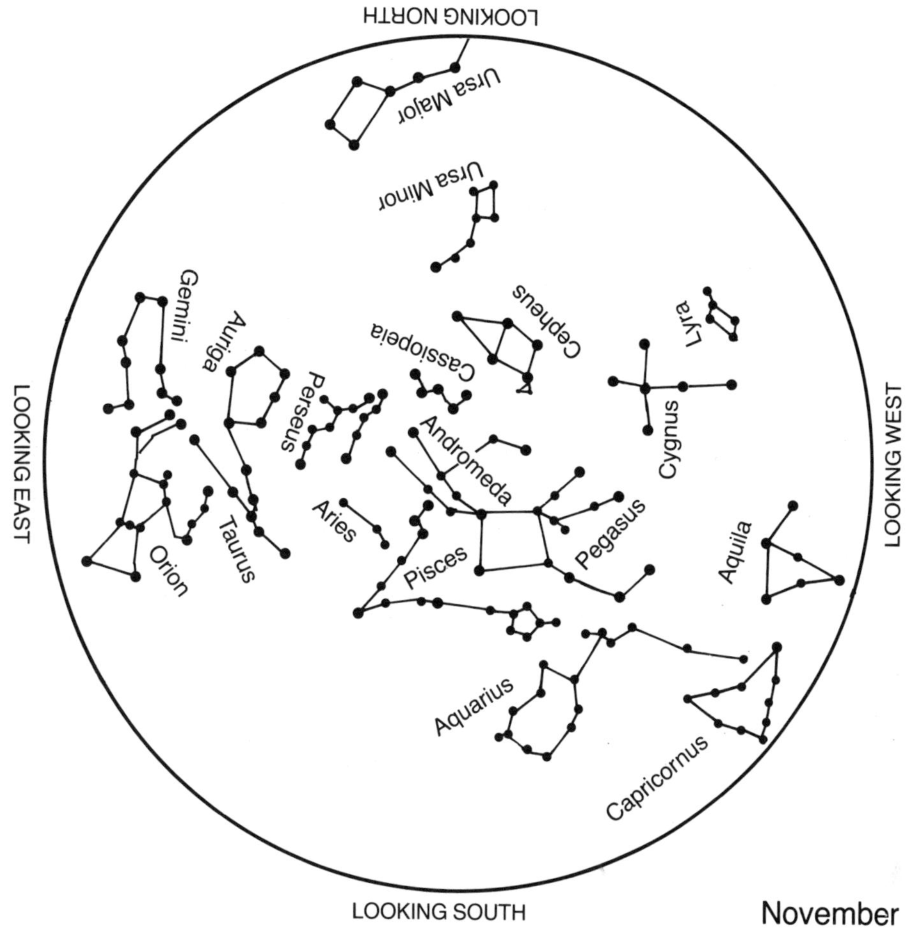

November

Square of Pegasus. Fum Al Samakah (fum-al-sa-MAK-a), "the fish's mouth," at the head of the Western Fish, is the second brightest star in the constellation. The Northern Fish, formed by a small triangle of stars, can be found by tracing along the line of stars that extends north from Al Rischa.

According to the Greeks, Aphrodite, the goddess of love, and her son,

Eros, were once walking along a river when they were attacked by the monster Typhon. To escape, they jumped into the water and were changed into fishes. From that time on, they have been seen as the Western and Northern Fishes of Pisces.

Cepheus (SEE-fee-us), the King, is a dim constellation of stars that you can find by facing north, turning slightly to the west, and looking up at an angle of about 60°. Its shape makes it easy to find. It resembles a square atop an equilateral triangle. The tip of the triangle points down to the northeast horizon. Above the upper righthand corner of the square (toward the south) is a small triangle made up of three stars representing the King's head. The square outlines his upper torso; the triangle, his royal robes.

The brightest star in Cepheus is Alderamin (al-DER-a-min), located near the King's right shoulder. At his right waist is Alfirk, the second brightest star in Cepheus. Just above Alderamin and the triangle of stars that forms the King's head is a reddish star, visible to the naked eye, that is called the Garnet Star. Seen through binoculars or a telescope, its color varies from very deep red to light orange.

And finally, be sure to search out the brightest and best known variable star in Cepheus, Delta Cephei (del-ta-SEE-fee-eye). Delta Cephei changes brightness in a regular pattern as its size and surface temperature rise and fall. Watch Delta Cephei for a few nights. Notice how it goes from bright to dim and back to bright about every five days.

Cepheus was the husband of Cassiopeia and the father of Andromeda. When an oracle demanded that Cepheus sacrifice Andromeda to Cetus, the sea monster, in order to protect his people, the King set aside his fatherly feelings and chained her to a rock. After he died, Cepheus became a constellation, but a faint and indistinct one.

Andromeda (an-DROM-e-duh), sometimes called the Chained Lady, is a constellation that is easily found near the northeast corner of the Great Square of Pegasus when looking south about 80° above the horizon. The picture usually shows a beautiful princess with her outspread arms chained to a rock. The star at the corner, you will recall, is Alpheratz, the bright "head-star" of Andromeda. Mirach (MY-rack), the second brightest star, marks the left waist of Andromeda. And Alamac, one of the faint stars, is found at her left leg.

To the north and slightly west of Mirach, you may be able to see a dim, glowing patch of light. It is another spiral galaxy like our own, the famous Andromeda Galaxy. But it is three times as large (about 300 billion stars), and is an estimated 2.2 million light-years away. As galaxies go, this galaxy, which is also called Andromeda Nebula, is considered a fairly close neighbor. Still, it is the most distant object visible to the naked eye.

As Cetus, the sea monster, was just about to devour Andromeda, Perseus arrived on his winged horse, Pegasus. He subdued the monster and rescued the terrified princess. In the autumn, you can see part of Perseus beside Andromeda in the northeast sky.

Cassiopeia (kass-ee-oh-PEE-ya), the Queen, is located at the side of her husband, Cepheus. To locate Cassiopeia, also called the Lady in Her Chair, look in the northern sky, about 70° above the horizon. Draw an imaginary line from Mizar, the second star in the handle of the Big Dipper, to Polaris, at the end of the Little Dipper handle. Continue the line about the same distance again to reach Cassiopeia's five main stars, which form a very clear but sprawling letter W in the sky. Cassiopeia and the Big Dipper slowly circle around Polaris throughout the year. For six months of the year the Queen sits on her throne head down; for the other six she is upright.

If you think of Cassiopeia as a seated figure, you will find her head at the

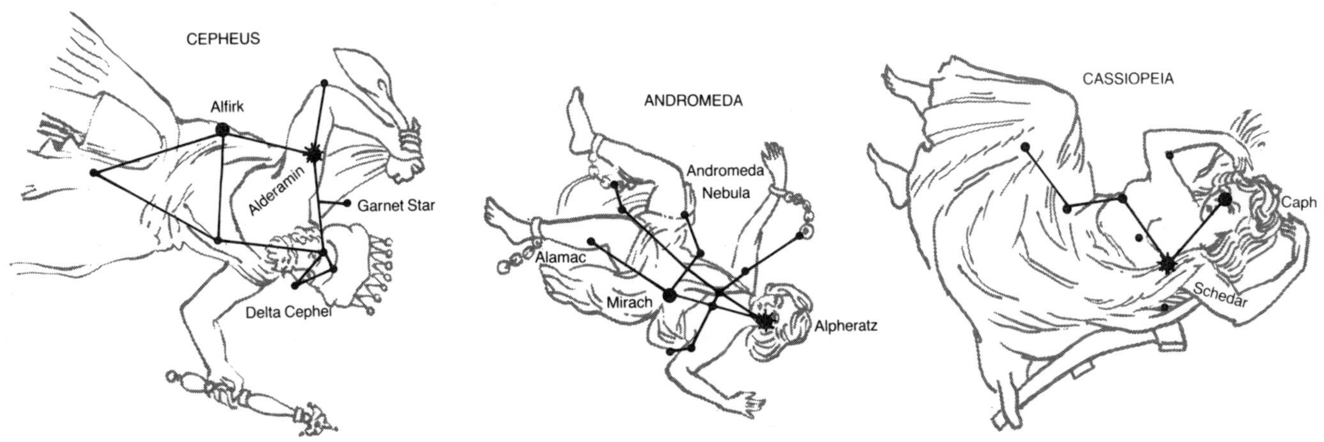

western end of the constellation. The second brightest star, Caph (KAFF), is found at her head; the brightest star, Schedar (SHED-er), at her breast. The rest of the stars outline her seated form.

The beautiful Cassiopeia, the ancient Greeks told, could not resist boasting of her daughter Andromeda's great beauty. One time she claimed that her daughter was even more lovely than the goddesses of the sea. This made the sea nymphs very angry so they decided to punish the vain Cassiopeia by changing her into a constellation. And to embarrass her and teach her to be modest, they placed her so that she sometimes appears to be resting on her head.

The Stars of December

Aries (AIR-eez), the Ram, is a small and faint constellation and the first sign of the zodiac. You can find Aries by looking just above 70° in the southern sky, and a little west of directly south. The constellation represents a ram with its head turned, looking back over its shoulder.

Three stars in a triangle form the ram's head. This includes the brightest star in Aries, Hamal (ha-MAL), from the Arabic meaning "head of the sheep," located near the ram's mouth. The second brightest star in Aries, Sheratan (SHER-a-tan), marks one horn of the ram.

According to the ancient Greeks, the ram with the golden fleece rescued the youth Phrixus from a death plot planned to prevent him from inheriting his father's kingdom. After saving Phrixus's life, the ram asked the youth to

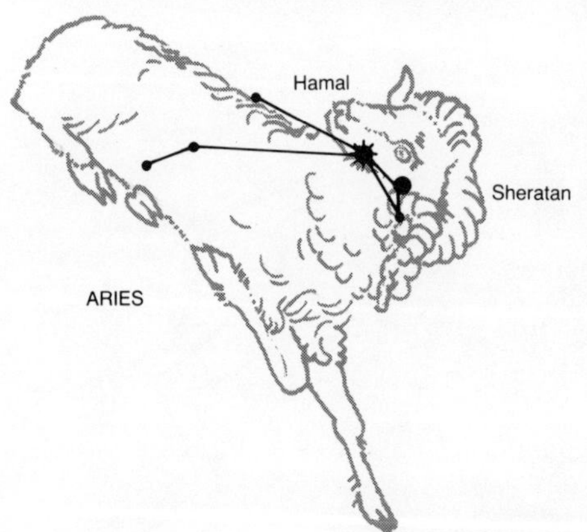

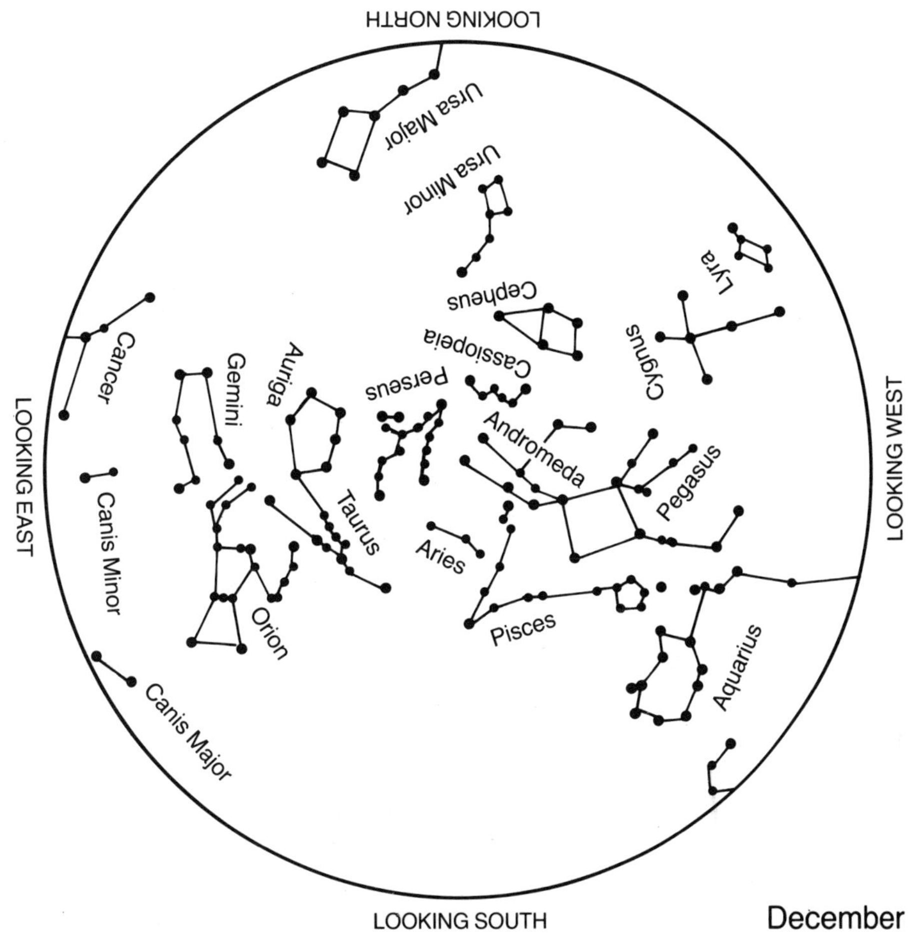

sacrifice him to the gods and make his golden fleece a gift to the King. The King received the present with great pleasure, rewarding the ram by giving it an eternal place in the sky.

Perseus (PUR-see-us), the Hero, comes into its best viewing position almost directly overhead in the northeast sky just before the end of Decem-

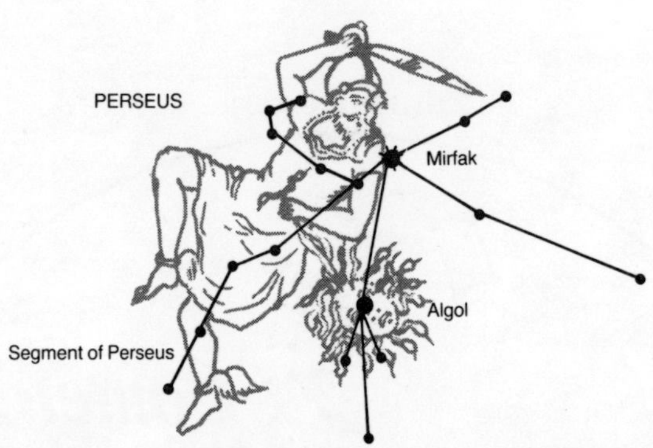

ber. A curved line of stars, called the Segment of Perseus, can be found to the west of Auriga, running southeast from Cassiopeia to Taurus.

Perseus, the son of Zeus, is usually shown as a young man. In his raised right hand he holds a sword; in his left, the head of Medusa whom he killed to save the chained Andromeda. In the Greek legend, Perseus did not dare to look at Medusa, who had snakes for hair and staring eyes that turned people to stone. But by using a shield as a mirror he was able to approach her, cut off her head and use the frightful sight to scare away Cetus, the sea monster, before he could devour Andromeda.

The best-known star of Perseus, found in the eye of Medusa's head, is Algol (AL-gol). The name comes from the Arabic word meaning "demon's head." Although Algol looks like a single twinkling star, astronomers have long known that it is a double star; an invisible companion star revolves around it, much as the moon revolves around the earth.

The two stars are located about 100 light-years away from earth. The effect of the companion star is to make Algol grow dimmer and brighter at regular intervals. For almost three days, we see Algol as a bright star. Then as the dark companion star circles between Algol and earth, it blocks our view and the light grows fainter for about five hours. The brightness subsequently increases for another five hours, as the darker star moves past Algol. After another three days or so, the process repeats itself. Each of Algol's slow "winks" in space takes about ten hours. Through one long night of winter you may want to watch an eclipse of Algol, the so-called Winking Demon. Remember, though, that the changes you see occurred a century ago.

2 / Comet Tracking

As you watch the skies, every once in a while you may notice an unusual object. Instead of being a sharp dot of light like a star, it is a fuzzy patch of gray in the sky. There may also be a "tail," a long stream of light coming from the object and stretching out through space. The ancient Greeks called such a heavenly body *aster kometes,* which means "hairy star." From the Greek name comes the term we use: comet.

Ancient skywatchers feared comets. They could not predict when they would appear or in what part of the sky they would be spotted because comets did not seem to follow orderly paths, like the sun, the other stars or the planets. They just appeared, traveled across the sky and disappeared into space. And, worst of all, almost every time a comet flashed into view, there would be a terrible calamity somewhere on earth, believed to be caused by the coming of the comet.

But as people began to understand what comets are, they stopped being afraid of these visitors from space. In fact, they became curious. Comet watchers sprang up everywhere. Some were professional astronomers, of course, but many were amateurs, who tracked them as a hobby. They tried to discover new comets, as well as to spot the return of known comets.

A comet appears as a fuzzy patch in the sky.

Among the best-known comet watchers was the French astronomer Jean Louis Pons. Between 1801 and 1827 he sighted thirty-seven new comets, a record number of discoveries. A retired English schoolteacher, George Alcock, is also famous. He observed the skies for 735 hours between 1959 and 1967, and found four comets not previously seen. And in Japan, Kaoru Ikeya, a worker in a piano factory, found one comet each year from 1963 to 1967. Of the six comets found in 1983, two were spotted by amateurs, three by professional astronomers and one by satellite.

Each year about six comets are visible in the night sky through telescopes or binoculars. But even if you have neither, you can still try your luck at comet tracking. After all, you may happen to find the one comet a year that can be seen with the naked eye. This may not seem like much compared to the thousands of stars that you can see every clear night, but the thrill of seeing—or of discovering—a comet makes it all worthwhile.

What Is a Comet?

An astronomer once described comets as "dirty snowballs." Every comet is indeed a solid ball of ice, called a nucleus. And imbedded in the nucleus are immense numbers of dust particles and bits of rock and metal. The nucleus may be anywhere from ½ to 30 miles in diameter.

Most of the time the comet is very, very far from the sun. Because the nucleus is so tiny and so distant, we cannot see it from earth.

Comets travel through vast orbits that take them from the outermost regions of the solar system inward, toward the sun. As the comet nucleus is exposed to the sun's heat, the ices in the nucleus change to a gas. This frees the dust particles; the gas and dust then form a huge cloud around the nucleus, called the coma. A coma may extend out as much as 600,000 miles beyond the nucleus and can take up more space than the sun itself. Together the nucleus and the coma make up the head of the comet.

Besides heat and light, the sun emits streams of subatomic particles, mostly protons and electrons, at great speeds and in all directions. These particles form the solar wind. This solar wind pushes on the coma, creating the long, thin tail of the comet. The tail, which looks like a streak of light coming from the comet, can be hundreds of millions of miles long—even longer than the distance between the earth and the sun.

Some comets move in an orbit known as an ellipse, a kind of egg-shaped, elongated circle. These comets are seen again and again at regular intervals. Other comets travel in U-shaped orbits (described in mathematics as parabolas); these are seen once and then disappear into the outermost regions of space.

To get a picture of an ellipse, attach a blank sheet of notebook paper to a bulletin board with two thumbtacks placed a few inches apart. Connect the tacks with a string loosely tied into a loop. Now, place your pencil inside the looped string and try to draw a circle around the two tacks. You'll find that the figure you draw is not a circle, but an ellipse.

If you want to visualize a parabola, do this simple experiment: Hold the two ends of a length of string with both hands. Hold your hands so that the string sags in the middle. The shape that the string takes is a parabola.

The comets that follow an ellipse in their orbit are known as periodic comets, a period being the length of time it takes a comet to make one complete orbit and return again to be seen from earth. Periodic comets travel in such immense elliptical orbits that they can take between 3 and 1,000 years to swoop around the sun. The comets that move in a parabolic orbit are nonperiodic; they pass near the sun—and earth—once, and then head away, never to return.

About seventy known comets have periods of 3 to 9 years; another forty take between 10 to 1,000 years to make a complete orbit. Of the estimated six comets sighted in the course of one year, two move along an ellipse (periodic) and four have parabolic orbits (nonperiodic).

Discovering Comets

Astronomers estimate that our solar system contains about 1 trillion comets. Of these, only about 1,300 have been sighted. The exact paths are known for fewer than 700. And we have detailed facts on a few dozen at most.

The great majority of comets are, therefore, still undetected. This is partly because they are hard to spot. And it is partly because many people do not know where or how to look for them. But if you have a spirit of adventure, you will probably love comet tracking. Like any adventure, its difficulty and challenge just make it more fun.

A bright comet can be a beautiful and awe-inspiring sight. It may be visible for a few days or for a few weeks. Visually, it will first appear as a fuzzy, gray patch in the dark night sky. The fuzzy appearance is sometimes confused with a nebula, a cloud of gas. Or it can look like a distant galaxy, a giant group or system of stars.

We know that the comet is hurtling through space at a speed of thousands of miles an hour. Yet, as you watch it, it does not appear to move at all because it is still so far away. But if you make observations over a few hours, or days, you may notice some movement. The closer the comet is to earth, the easier it is to see its motion through the sky.

The tail, as mentioned earlier, develops as the solar wind pushes on the gas molecules and dust particles in the head of the comet. When the comet is heading toward the sun, the pressure makes the tail extend behind the comet, that is, away from the sun. When the comet is moving away from the sun, though, something strange happens: The tail actually moves in front of, or to the side of, the comet.

When closest to the sun, the comet becomes quite bright. The brightness comes from the reflected light of the sun and is also the result of the sun causing some atoms in the comet to glow and give off their own light.

Even at their brightest, comets are not among the most brilliant objects in the sky. For this reason, it is best to comet-watch on a night when there are very few clouds and little moonlight. Also, try to comet-watch on nights following a rainstorm when the sky is often particularly clear. It is best, too, to watch away from artificial lights on earth. Be sure, though, to give your eyes time to become adjusted to the dark.

Comets are best seen when they are near the sun. Therefore, look in the western sky just after sunset or in the eastern sky just before dawn. Statistics show that almost three times as many comets have been sighted in the few hours before sunrise or just after sunset than at any other time. If you are really serious about viewing comets, you may have to set an alarm and get up by four or five o'clock in the morning. This may not be as hard as it sounds, because the largest numbers of comet discoveries are made during the warm months of July and August.

You may want to follow the system for discovering comets that most comet hunters use. Divide the sky into four sections—north, west, south, east. Facing in one direction, sweep your eyes back and forth slowly just over the horizon line. If you don't detect anything unusual, move your eyes up one level. Again, sweep back and forth at that height. After you've completely covered that part of the sky, make a quarter turn to your right. Start again at the horizon and move up slowly. Repeat until you have covered the entire sky.

If you think you have spotted a new comet, there are several steps you should take: First, jot down the location of the object. Note the direction you were facing when you made the observation. Estimate the comet's altitude over the horizon and give the name of the constellation in which the comet is located.

Next, go indoors and consult a star chart to see if there is a nebula or a galaxy at the comet's location in the sky. Be sure that you have not been misled by the resemblances between a nebula or a galaxy and a far-off comet. If what you have sighted still seems to be a comet, look up your sighting in a magazine such as *Astronomy* or *Sky and Telescope*. Often, you will find a chart in these magazines that gives the path and location (called ephemeris) of periodic comets visible from earth.

If your comet is not listed on any ephemeris, you may indeed have spotted a new comet. Astronomers worldwide are interested in the discovery of new comets, therefore, you should get in touch with the international clearinghouse that coordinates all comet sightings. To do this, telegram, call or write:

Central Bureau for Astronomical Telegrams
Smithsonian Astrophysical Observatory
Cambridge, MA 02134
(617) 864-5758

The information you give should include the approximate position of the comet, the date and time of the observation, a description of the comet (including its brightness and whether a tail was visible) and your full name, address and telephone number.

If you have really made a finding, the Central Bureau will help you to identify it properly. They will tag the comet with the year and number of discovery for that period. For example, Comet 1985c means the third comet (since c is the third letter of the alphabet) found in 1985. Later, if it turns out that you were the first to see the comet, it will be named after you or after any others (one to three) who saw it at about the same time. A well-known example of a comet discovered by three people at the same time is the Comet Tuttle-Giacobini-Kresak.

Rediscovering Comets

You may prefer to look for known comets because your chances of finding them are greater than of spotting new ones. Also, there is plenty of information to help you locate returning periodic comets.

The chart below lists the predicted returns of comets during the years 1985 through 1999. It includes only the brightest comets, the ones you are most apt to spot with your eyes alone. (For more exact data and ephemerides, consult current issues of *Astronomy* or *Sky and Telescope.)*

COMET NAME	*YEAR*	*MONTH*
Honda-Mrkos-Pajdusakova	1985	May
Giacobini-Zinner	1985	September
Halley	1986	April
Encke	1987	July
Klemola	1987	July
Reinmuth 2	1987	October
Reinmuth 1	1988	May
Tempel 2	1988	September
Schwassmann-Wachmann 1	1989	October
Encke	1990	October
Encke	1994	February
Tempel 2	1994	March
Encke	1997	May

Halley's Comet

Halley's is the most famous of all periodic comets. This well-known comet orbits the sun about once every 76 years, although it may arrive up to two years earlier or three years later. Comet Halley follows a giant elliptical course through the solar system. It can be seen from the earth only as it nears the sun. Astronomers believe it was first sighted by Chinese stargazers in 240 B.C.

The comet is named for English astronomer Edmund Halley (1656-1742), who was the first to predict that some comets travel in definite paths around the sun at regular intervals. He guessed that the comet that appeared in 1682

This photograph was taken during Halley's 1910 passage near earth.

was the same one that had appeared in 1456, 1531 and 1607. Halley also forecast that the comet would reappear in 1759—which it did—and at regular intervals after that.

In 1910 the comet once again approached the sun, and was seen as a brilliant, awesome sight in the heavens. On this occasion, for the first time, astronomers were able to photograph the comet. They studied these photographs very carefully. The nucleus, they found, had a diameter of about 3 miles. The surrounding coma extended out for some 250,000 miles. And the great tail, stretched out like a huge streak across the sky, was nearly 100 million miles long.

Latter-day astronomers look forward to Halley's next showing, which will be its twenty-ninth recorded appearance. They have worked out a timetable and viewing suggestions for this return of Halley's Comet:

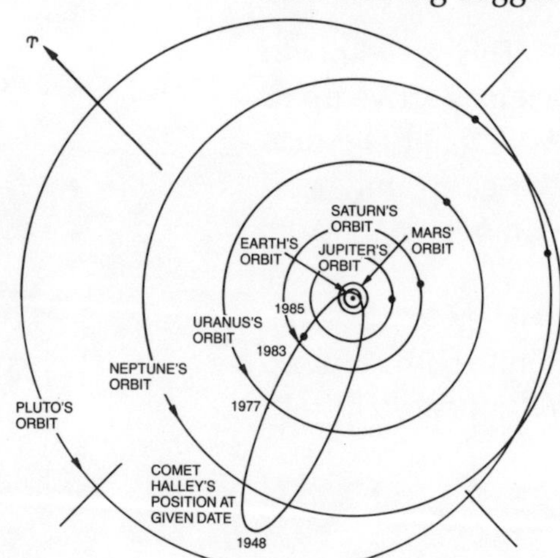

1948 Halley is at its farthest point (nearly 33 billion miles) from the sun, called the aphelion, located in the most distant reaches of the solar system, between the orbits of Neptune and Pluto. At this point, the sun's gravity spins the comet around, starting it on its trip back toward the sun at a speed of about 5,000 miles per hour.

October 16, 1982 Through a powerful telescope on earth, astronomers catch the first glimpse of the returning comet. It is still 2½ billion miles away, beyond the planet Saturn, but moving faster and faster toward the earth and sun.

November 27, 1985 Halley is only 58 million miles from earth, the closest approach on its inward-bound trip. As it hurtles toward the sun, it picks up speed, traveling at over 300,000 miles per hour. Still invisible to the naked eye, the comet can be seen with telescopes passing through the constellation Taurus, between Aldebaran and the Pleiades.

January 5, 1986 For the first time, Halley is visible through binoculars or the naked eye, starting about one hour after sunset. It appears at a height of about 30° in the western sky in a southerly direction. On each succeeding night for the month of January, it shows up lower in the sky and more toward the west.

February 9, 1986 Halley is at perihelion, closest to the sun on this day, which blocks its view from earth. After making a loop around the sun, the comet starts its long voyage away from the sun and back toward the outer reaches of the solar system.

March 1986 Starting at the beginning of this month, Halley can be seen in the early morning hours, about an hour before sunrise. You see it low in the sky to the southwest. At first it comes into view at horizon level. On March 6th its altitude is about 5°; it reaches its greatest height in the sky, around 10°, on March 26.

April 5, 1986 Halley is its brightest and most visible on this day.

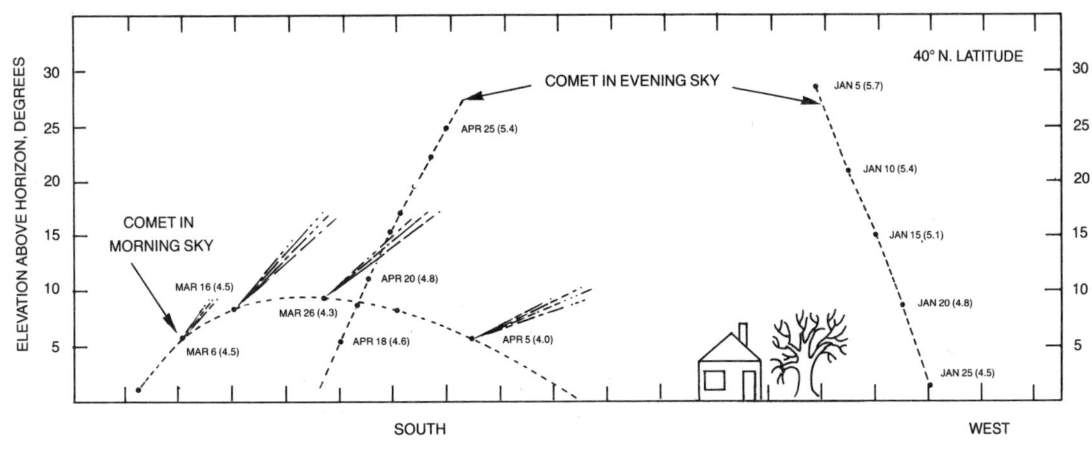

Viewing is best in the few hours just before sunrise. The comet is found almost directly south, and is low in the sky, only 5° above the horizon.

April 11, 1986 The comet comes closest to earth, less than 40 million miles distant.

April 18, 1986 Now begins the final week of naked-eye observation. The comet is best seen just after sunset, facing south. On this day of the month, Halley is low in the sky, just about 5° above the horizon and toward the east. With each passing day, it reaches a higher level and moves more directly south.

July 1987 Astronomers take their last looks at Halley through their telescopes as the comet speeds off into space.

2024 Comet Halley is again at its aphelion, the farthest distance from the sun. This marks the start of its trip back to the center of the solar system.

2062 Halley returns to earth, about 76 years after its last visit in 1986, and its thirtieth sighting since 240 B.C.

Meteors

Early in May 1986, after Halley has faded from naked-eye view, you may see brilliant flashes of light sweep across the night sky. Some people call such objects shooting stars or falling stars. The fact is that they have nothing at all to do with stars. They are actually tiny bits of matter from the nucleus of Comet Halley. In May 1986 the planet earth actually passes near Halley's orbit, some seven weeks after the comet has flown by.

Like other comets, Halley is not very neat and tidy. As it travels along its path, it leaves a trail of tiny particles of matter. These particles, which resemble grains of sand, are called meteoroids. (Larger meteoroids come from collisions between asteroids.) The comet's meteoroids are much too small to be seen. But when they enter the earth's atmosphere, they become white-hot as a result of friction with the molecules that make up the air.

Meteoroids travel at very high speeds, about 26 miles per second, nearly 100,000 miles per hour. As they dive into the atmosphere, they strip electrons from the molecules in the air. This causes their path in the air, about 50 to 75 miles above earth, to glow. The result is a streak of light, called a meteor.

You can see meteors on almost any dark night. If you watch for an hour, you should spot between five and ten meteors on the average.

The best time to view meteors is between midnight and sunrise. Astronomers estimate the number to be almost twice as great as before midnight. The reason is that between 12 A.M. and 6 A.M. you are on the forward-facing part of the earth as it moves around the sun. You see all the meteors that the earth overtakes, as well as those meteors traveling fast enough to catch up with our planet. Before midnight you only see those meteors that move fast enough to overtake earth. It is like running in the rain; more raindrops strike the front of your body than strike your back.

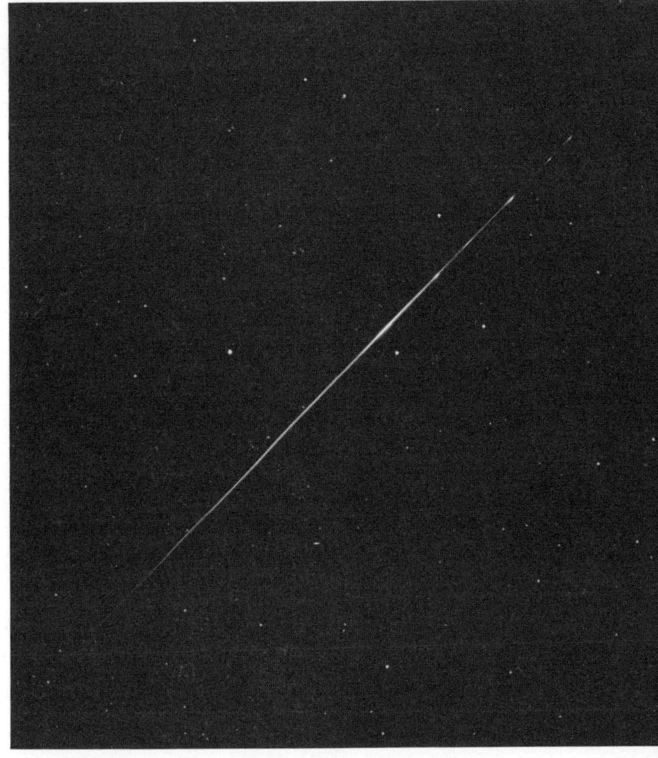

A meteor leaves a bright trail across the night sky.

Meteor Showers

When earth passes near or through the path of a large comet, the number of meteors that are visible rises dramatically. In one hour of observing you may see fifty or more. Such displays are called meteor showers.

You will often find that all the streaks you see during a meteor shower seem to be coming from one spot or area of the sky. Astronomers call this point of origin the radiant. Actually, the radiant is an optical illusion. The meteors *seem* to be coming from the same place because they are so far away (like two parallel railroad tracks that appear to converge in the distance).

Meteor showers take their names from the constellations in which their radiants are found. The early May meteor shower that follows Halley's

Comet, for example, is known as the Eta Aquarids because its radiant is found in the constellation Aquarius.

Below is a table of some well-known meteor showers, indicating their dates, names, location of radiant and approximate number of meteors seen per hour:

DATE	***NAME***	***CONSTELLATION***	***NUMBER PER HOUR***
Jan. 1–4	*Quadrantids*	*Boötes (named after an old constellation but now in Boötes)*	*50*

These meteors have a faint bluish color. The best way to see them is to face northeast and look almost directly overhead.

Apr. 19–24	*Lyrids*	*Lyra*	*10*

The number of meteors in this shower has been decreasing since they were first sighted in 687 B.C. The radiant is near the bright star Vega in Lyra. It is directly overhead at about 11:00 P.M.

May 1–6	*Eta Aquarids*	*Aquarius*	*20*

These meteors are the debris from Halley's Comet. They are usually bright yellow in color and leave bright, glowing trails.

July 26–31	*Delta Aquarids*	*Aquarius*	*25*

Most of these meteors can be seen in the south sky after midnight.

July 25–Aug. 18	*Perseids*	*Perseus*	*50*

Considered the finest of the meteor showers. After midnight on a clear, dark night you might see as many as one-hundred per hour. Some seem to explode, sending several meteors shooting out from the main one.

Oct. 18–23	*Orionids*	*Orion*	*20*

The clear, crisp October skies make the Orionids particularly easy to see. These fast-moving meteors are traveling at speeds as great as 40,000 miles per hour.

Oct. 20–Nov. 30 Taurids Taurus 10

The Taurids include a number of especially bright meteors. Those that emit so much light that they cast a shadow on earth are known as fireballs.

Nov. 14–18 Leonids Leo 20

The radiant of the Leonids is in the sickle, or question mark, of Leo. Every thirty-three years the number of meteors reaches a peak, providing a spectacular display. At the last peak, on November 16, 1966, naked-eye observers made over 10,000 sightings per hour. The next peak, in 1999, should be just as exciting.

Dec. 10–13 Geminids Gemini 60

Although most of the meteors of the Geminids are quite bright, only a few leave a trail in the sky. They can be seen overhead at about midnight.

Astronomers depend to some extent on amateur observers to help them gather information on meteor activity. Even if you are a beginner, your findings may be of value.

Here is how to go about making meteor observations: Trace the star chart for the right month on a piece of paper. Take it outdoors clipped to a clipboard or attached to a cardboard. Bring along a pencil, a flashlight with a red filter and a watch.

Each time you see a meteor flash do the following on your star chart:

1. Draw a line in the appropriate place on the chart showing the meteor track from start to finish. Put an arrow at one end to indicate the direction of movement.

2. Count off the seconds (one-one thousand, two-one thousand, etc.) from appearance to disappearance. Enter the duration of the meteor in a lower corner of the chart.

3. Give the exact time of the meteor in Universal Time (UT). UT works on the 24-hour clock. One A.M. is 1, noon is 12, 1 P.M. is 13, midnight is 24. To determine UT from standard time, convert it to the 24-hour clock, and add 5

for Eastern Standard Time, 6 for Central Standard Time, 7 for Mountain Standard Time and 8 for Pacific Standard Time. (Suppose you live in Atlanta, Georgia, and sight a meteor at 5:12 A.M. by your watch, which would normally be set to Eastern Standard Time. That also happens to be 5:12 on the 24-hour clock. To get UT, though, you must add 5 hours. The time, then, is 10:12 UT.) To change daylight saving time to UT, subtract one hour from standard time. Enter the precise UT of observation above the line you have drawn.

4. Measure the meteor train with your fingers. Hold your right arm straight out, palm facing left, fingers straight. Then turn your fingers toward you so that their width (without the thumb) covers the meteor track. Using only one eye, see how many fingers it takes to cover the track. The width of each finger is equal to about 4°. A trail that can be covered with three fingers, for example, is about 12° long. Enter the length in degrees in the corner of the chart.

5. Describe the color and brightness of the front part of the meteor, not its tail. Rank the brightness on a scale from 1 to 5; 1 being as bright as the brightest star in the sky whose position you can describe.

6. Mention any unusual behavior, such as a change in direction, a striking color, an explosion and breaking apart, a sputtering trail, etc.

7. Keep an hourly count, if possible. Mark each meteor you see on the chart. Divide the observations into 15-minute periods, labelled according to UT. Later, you can use the figures to find the peak of activity of this meteor shower.

You can send your observations to the agency that collects and files this information:

American Meteor Society
Department of Physics and Astronomy
SUNY Geneseo
Geneseo, NY 14454

Meteorites

About 20 million meteoroids enter the earth's atmosphere every day. Many of them produce the streaks of light that we call meteors. Almost all drift down to earth as fine dust. Astronomers estimate that this dust adds about 4,000 pounds to the mass of the earth every 24 hours.

In all this material that rains down on earth, however, are a few objects that are larger than grain-size. Some are at least 8 inches in diameter and look stonelike. These objects that fall to earth from outer space are known as meteorites.

Meteorites can be grouped into three kinds: irons, which are mostly iron with perhaps 10 percent nickel; stones, which are mostly mineral, like earth rock; and stony-irons, which are a mixture of iron and rock-like minerals.

If you find a rocklike, metallic object far from an iron mine or other likely source, it may be a meteorite. To test the object, hold it to a magnet. A substance that attracts the magnet probably contains metal.

This iron meteorite is about one foot long.

Next, compare the weight of this object with the weight of a rock of about the same size; meteorites are generally a great deal heavier than similar-sized earth rocks. To make certain you have a meteorite, take or send the object to a planetarium or to the geology department of a nearby college or museum. The experts there can perform chemical tests that will prove whether or not you have found a meteorite.

Who can say if it is more thrilling to see a comet hurtling through space, or to hold a lost part of one such object in your hand? Fortunately, you don't have to make a choice. With comet tracking, you may be able to have it all.

3 / Sky Mapping

Star gazing and comet tracking are both fascinating activities. But there is even more that you can do in astronomy. In this section are directions on how to prepare your own sky maps, measure various objects in space and demonstrate some of the basic laws of science. Here, too, are ways to tell time by the sun and other stars.

All the projects described below require materials that can either be found around the house or are inexpensive to buy. With your homemade gadgets and devices, you will have tools that will help you get to know the sky better. What's more, these instruments will come in handy if you decide to tackle more ambitious astronomical observations later on.

Building a Star Plotter

A simple star plotter will let you map or chart the positions of the stars in the sky as you see them. To build a plotter, you'll need to gather together some very simple materials. Find or buy from a home repair store a 12-inch square (1/8- or 1/4-inch thick) piece of hard, clear plastic, such as Lucite or Plexiglas. The positions of the stars will be plotted on this plastic. You'll also need a strip of wood about 6 inches long, 1 inch wide and 1/2 inch

thick to serve as the plotter's handle.

Drill two 1/4-inch holes near the center of one end of the plastic, about 1/2 inch from the edge. Use wood screws to attach the handle to the plastic sheet.

When you are ready to use your star plotter, take it outside. You'll need a light-colored grease pencil to mark the stars on the plastic.

Figure out a way to brace the hand holding the plotter against something so that it is steady. Perhaps you can rest it against a post, a tree or some other fixed object. Or you can prop your hand on the top of a long stick, such as a broomstick, that you set on the ground.

Now point your plotter at some part of the sky that looks rich with stars. In a corner of the plastic, mark down the following basic data with the grease pencil: the direction (north, south, east or west) of your observation, the angle above the horizon (30°, 45°, 60° or whatever), the date and the hour.

Next, make a little dot in the proper place on the plastic for each object that you see. Make the dots a little bigger for the brighter objects, a little smaller for those that are less bright.

After you have made the pattern of dots, take the plotter indoors. Tape tracing paper over the plastic. Trace the stars you have marked. Also copy onto the paper the information on direction, angle, date and hour of the viewing. When you have traced everything from the plotter to the paper, wipe the plastic clean with a soft rag.

Now you are ready to make another map. Perhaps this time you will want to plot the stars in another section of the sky. Or you may want to wait a few hours and then map the same part again to see how the positions of the stars have changed. Perhaps you will start a series of maps showing the same area over different months of the year. This will let you follow the stars' movement over long periods of time. If you keep at it, you will soon have an excellent set of sky charts that are correct for your exact latitude on earth.

Charting the Constellations

Most star charts that show the constellations include just their main stars. They leave out the surrounding stars in order to make the constellation stand out more clearly. With your star plotter, though, you can prepare star charts showing the constellations and the other stars as they actually appear in the sky.

Before you begin to map the constellations, consult the proper monthly star chart in this book. Then turn your plotter to the direction and altitude of one of the visible constellations.

Once you have found the stars that make up that constellation, move your plotter so that they appear near the center of the plastic. Now mark the stars of the constellation with your grease pencil, making the dots larger for the brighter stars. Include as many of the stars around the figure of the constellation as you can. Also, be sure to write in the direction, angle, date and hour of your observation.

The next step is to make a tracing on paper of all the stars on the plotter. Connect the main constellation stars in a pattern similar to the one shown in this book. Finally, label your chart with the name of the constellation. Check to see that you have copied over the date and hour of the observation, the direction you were facing and the altitude of the constellation center. You can now make your own collection of drawings of the different constellations.

Making a Photo Map

With your own camera or a borrowed one, you can make photographic maps of the different parts of the sky. The best camera you can use includes controls that allow you to adjust the lens opening, the shutter speed and the focusing distance.

You should set the lens to its maximum opening. The opening is measured in f-stops; the lower the f-number, the larger the opening of the lens.

For the shutter speed, there is no hard and fast rule. It varies with the size of the lens opening, the type of film you use and the brightness of the stars you are photographing. Generally, the exposure time should range between 10 seconds and 1 minute. Less than 10 seconds, and you won't be able to pick up the fainter stars on the film; more than a minute and you may begin to get a blur as the earth moves in relation to the stars in space.

The final control you set is the focusing distance. Adjust the focusing scale to the longest distance, which is usually marked "Infinity." This will make objects at great distances from the camera—such as the stars—reasonably well-focused and sharp in appearance.

Use black-and-white film for photographing the night sky. Any one of the so-called fast films will provide good results. Kodak's Plus-X and Tri-X are two such films, but there are several others available.

A tripod is necessary for taking sky photos, since it is difficult to hold a camera steady for more than a tiny fraction of a second. If you do not have a tripod and cannot borrow one, place and hold the camera on a solid surface while shooting. For especially good results, use a cable release, if one is available. This eliminates the camera jiggle caused by pressing the shutter release.

Think of the first roll of film you shoot—say a 20-exposure roll—as experimental. Photograph the same view with different settings. In particular try it with different exposure lengths. Take one or two pictures with exposures less than 10 seconds. Then shoot with much longer exposures, going up to 5, 10 and even 15 minutes. Be sure to keep very careful records of each shot. After the film is developed and printed, the records will help you learn from your mistakes.

Once you know how to snap good sky pictures, you can produce general survey photo maps that will provide broad views of the night sky. Plan to take four photos of the sky, one after another, facing in each of the directions and aiming at an altitude of about 45°. This will give you a large slice of the sky. Then, approximately one month later, take a similar set of four photos. When you get the prints, enter the important information on the back with a grease pencil or felt-tipped pen. Include the date and hour of the picture, the direction, any constellations that are visible, the film, exposure length and other details of the actual photo. Do not use a ballpoint pen or lead pencil, since they will leave marks on the photo surface.

You can also photograph special objects in the sky the same way. Some shutterbugs aim the camera so that Polaris is in the exact center of the frame. This gives them a picture of the stars around that important skymark. Can you think of other sky features you might capture on film?

A "Handy" Way to Make Sky Measurements

To locate a star or constellation, you need to know how far up it is over the horizon. Or you need the distance—up or down or from side to side—from some other fixed object in space.

These measurements are too immense to be given in miles. They are usually given in degrees.

As you probably know, there are 360° in a circle. When you face north and turn completely around until you are facing north again, you have turned 360°. When you do a somersault and end up facing the same way you started, you've gone 360°.

We mentioned before that we call the horizon 0°. If you look straight overhead, then you're turned 90°. It is 90° because you have moved one quarter of the way around a circle, and 360° divided by 4 equals 90°.

A complete about-face in direction is 180°. It is halfway around a circle (360° divided by 2 equals 180°). Therefore, from north to south and from east to west are both 180° turns.

It's easy to measure 360° (a full circle), 90° (a quarter circle) and 180° (a half circle). But how do you make the in-between measurements?

There is a very old—and "handy"—way to measure distances in space. Here's how it works: Extend both hands straight out, palms facing each other. Tuck both thumbs in against the palms. Hold the other four fingers together. Then turn your hands so that you can see the inside of your fingers and the fingertips of one hand touch the fingertips of the other. The span of the four fingers from top to bottom is about 15°.

You may be thinking, "Children have thinner fingers than grown-ups.

How can everyone's fingers always measure 15°?" The explanation is that grown-ups also tend to have longer arms than children; they hold their hands farther away. And the farther away, the smaller the apparent size. Therefore, the children's fingers *appear* the same size as the adults' fingers.

Let's try a finger-measurement experiment. Suppose you want to find a star that is 15° above the horizon. Stretch one hand out so that you can see the horizon just beneath the side of your little finger. Then 15° higher is just above the side of your top finger.

Now imagine you want to measure a distance that's more than 15°. How could you find a constellation that is 30° above the horizon? First, face in the direction of the constellation. Hold one hand out in front of you with the bottom side of your little finger at the horizon level. Without moving that hand, place the four fingers of your other hand above it, resting the second hand on the first. Since each hand equals 15°, the two hands make up a total of 30°. The top of the second hand is at the 30° height or altitude.

How do you measure distances smaller than 15°? For example, how would you find a star that is 8° to the east of another star? You know that the four fingers of one hand equal 15°. Therefore, each finger is slightly less than 4° (15° divided by 4 equals 3.75°, which can be rounded out to 4°). To measure 8°, hold up just two fingers. If you move your hand so that the original star is seen alongside one finger, the star you are seeking should be on the opposite side of the other finger.

Once you know this "handy" way to measure distances, you can use it to help find the stars and constellations shown on the printed charts. You may also want to add the altitude figure, in degrees, to the star charts you prepare.

Mapping the Sky by Astrolabe

Hand measurements can only give approximate figures. They don't produce very accurate results. To make more exact measurements, you can build an observing instrument called an astrolabe.

For supplies, you'll need two pieces of scrap lumber, each about 12 inches long, 1/2 inch thick and 1/2 inch wide. Place the center of one just beneath the top of the other so that they form the letter T. Drill a 1/4-inch hole through both pieces of wood. Insert a 1/4-inch bolt and wing nut. The cross stick is the sighting stick; the upright is the support stick. Tighten the nut enough to keep the two sticks in place, but loose enough so that you can tilt the sighting stick.

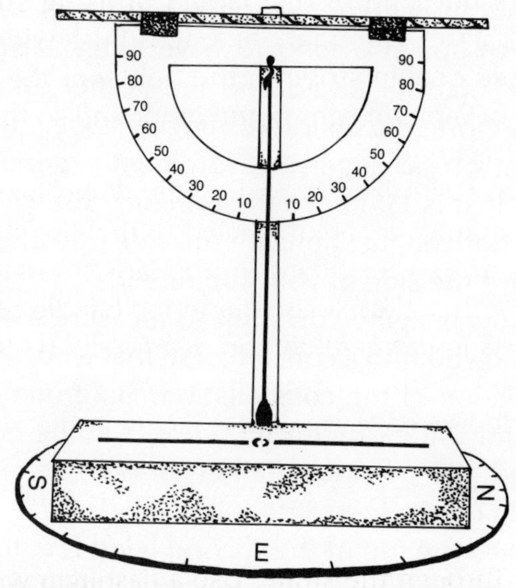

Next nail a protractor to the sighting stick. Place it on the side opposite the spot where the sighting stick is attached to the support stick. The protractor should be positioned so that the exact center of its flat base touches the bolt.

For the base of your astrolabe you'll need a piece of 1-inch-thick wood about 6 inches long and 3 inches wide. Nail the bottom of the support stick to the middle of one of the 6-inch sides.

Get a heavy piece of cardboard next. Cut out a 12-inch circle. Divide the circle into quarters by drawing two lines at right angles through the center. Mark north, east, south and west around the edge where each of the lines end. Divide the distance between the directions into three equal parts. Each of these marks represents 30°. Drill a hole through the exact center of the base block and through the center of the cardboard. Use a large metal paper fastener to attach the cardboard to the bottom of the base.

Draw a line through the center of the length of the top of the base.

Mark one end north. Tape a drinking straw along the top of the sighting stick. Place it so that one end is flush with an end of the sighting stick. Tie a thread or thin string to the bolt over the center of the protractor. Attach a key or other weight to the other end so that the thread hangs down over the protractor.

Your astrolabe is now ready to be used. Take it outside. Place it on an absolutely flat, level surface so that the straw is at eye level.

Your first task is to find Polaris, the North Star, through the straw. You recall that it is the last star in the handle of the Little Dipper. (Look at the sky charts in this book if you need help in locating the Little Dipper.) Polaris is always to the north. Therefore, once you have found the star, turn the cardboard so that north is facing in that direction.

Now you're set. Find a bright star by eye alone, without using the astrolabe. Then, without moving the cardboard, turn the astrolabe to face in that direction. Next, tilt the sighting stick up or down until you can see the star through the straw. Use a flashlight with a red filter over the lens to see which way the line on the base is pointing. That tells you the direction, and how many degrees it is away from due north. Then see where the thread crosses the protractor. That tells you the angle, or the altitude above the horizon.

The astrolabe will help you locate the constellations and will enable you to prepare your own sky maps, with each major star in the exact spot it is seen from your particular latitude.

Measuring the Sun's Altitude

When you think about stars and constellations it is easy to forget that the sun is also a star. It does not look like any other star because it is so much closer to earth. That makes for one important difference: You can stare at the distant stars and constellations for hours without damaging your eyes. Yet you dare not look at the sun, even for an instant, because it can cause permanent harm.

Since you can't look at the sun, how can you measure its altitude? The sun's altitude is of interest because it changes with the seasons. It is at its highest point, 73°, on June 21st, the first day of summer. For the rest of the summer and the autumn it grows lower. The lowest point, 27°, comes on December 21st, the first day of winter. Over the winter and spring months it rises until it is summer again.

You can chart the sun's altitude in this way: You'll need a straight stick or dowel 6 to 30 inches long, a protractor, a length of string, paper and a pencil to make a record of your findings.

Either place the stick straight up in the ground or attach it upright to a flat board. Attach the string to the top of the stick with a tack or tape.

Make your observations sometime between 11:30 A.M. and 12:30 P.M. See where the tip of the stick's shadow falls and attach the other end of the string at that point, either by tack or tape. Once it is secured, hold the protractor with the center of its base where the bottom of the string is attached. Measure the angle of the string with the protractor. Enter the date and the angle on the paper.

Repeat this experiment on several different days. Is the angle growing larger or smaller? The figures can tell you the season of the year. If the angle is near 27° and rising, it is winter. If the angle is increasing and approaching 73°, it is spring. A falling angle near 73° indicates summer. But if the angle is dropping near 27°, it is autumn.

Measuring the Sun's Size

Without looking at the sun, we can measure its size in a clever way.

Get an empty cardboard box, such as a shoebox. Remove the top of the box and cut a hole about 1-inch square near the middle of one of the smaller sides. Tape a piece of aluminum foil over the hole, and poke a pinhole through the center of the foil.

Place the box so that the pinhole faces the sun. You will see the round image of the sun on the inside of the box's opposite small panel. Measure the diameter of that image and enter that figure on a piece of paper.

Next, measure the distance from the pinhole to the image. That is, measure from the outside of the pinhole panel to the inside of the image panel. Write that number down, too.

Now, here is the formula by which you can find the diameter of the sun. It is really a ratio: The diameter of the image is to the distance from the pinhole to the image as the diameter of the sun is to the distance from sun to earth. In equation form it can be written thus:

$$\frac{\textit{Diameter of image (in inches)}}{\textit{Distance from pinhole to image (in inches)}} = \frac{\textit{Diameter of sun (in miles)}}{\textit{Distance from sun to earth (in miles)}}$$

The distance from the sun to earth is approximately 93 million miles. Therefore, to solve this equation, you multiply the diameter of the image by 93,000,000. Then divide the result by the distance from the pinhole to the image. The answer is the diameter of the sun. It should be around 870,000 miles.

You can measure the moon's diameter in the same way. The next night there is a full, or nearly full, moon, point the pinhole at the moon and measure the diameter of the image. Multiply that number by 240,000, the distance in miles from earth to moon. Then divide the result by the distance from pinhole to image. This will give you the diameter of the moon. Your answer should be around 2,000 miles.

Counting Stars

We said before that experienced observers can see about 3,000 stars under ideal viewing conditions—on a clear, dark night, and far from the glow of cities, buildings or car lights.

Would you like to know how many stars you can see? Here's an easy way to get a count. Using a tube on which paper toweling or aluminum foil is wrapped, go outside on a good night for star gazing and wait a few minutes for your eyes to get accustomed to the dark. Then look up through the tube at any point in the sky. Count the number of stars you can see through the tube, then write down the number. Next, look in a different direction and copy the number of stars you see this time. Repeat this a total of ten times.

Add the total number of stars you saw in your observations; divide the number by 10. This gives you the average number you saw each time. Multiply the average by the formula number, 700. The figure you get is approximately the number you would see if you counted every visible star. Is it close to 3,000?

Observing the Motion of the Sky

From earth, the sky seems to be moving all the time. That is because we live on a spinning globe. Although we never feel ourselves being whirled around, we see the effects of the motion as we look up to the sky. The heavens always appear to be in motion, from east to west, carrying the sun, moon, planets and stars with them.

The earth, we know, rotates on its north–south axis. An imaginary sphere that surrounds earth and carries all the celestial objects with it appears to rotate around the same axis. It is called the celestial sphere. In the exact center of the northern celestial sphere is the celestial north pole.

To demonstrate the earth's rotation and to capture a star trail, you need the same equipment you used to make the photo maps. Point the lens at Polaris, which is very near the actual celestial north pole. Leave the shutter open for 5 minutes. Then take other shots at 10-, 15-, 30-minute and even longer exposures.

Keep a careful record of the length of time for each picture. Then, after developing and printing the film, decide which exposure time works best. The pictures should show a series of circular light trails as the stars track across the sky.

Take a very careful look at your pictures. Do they show the apparent rotation of the sky? If so, can you tell the direction of rotation? What does it tell you about the rotation of the earth?

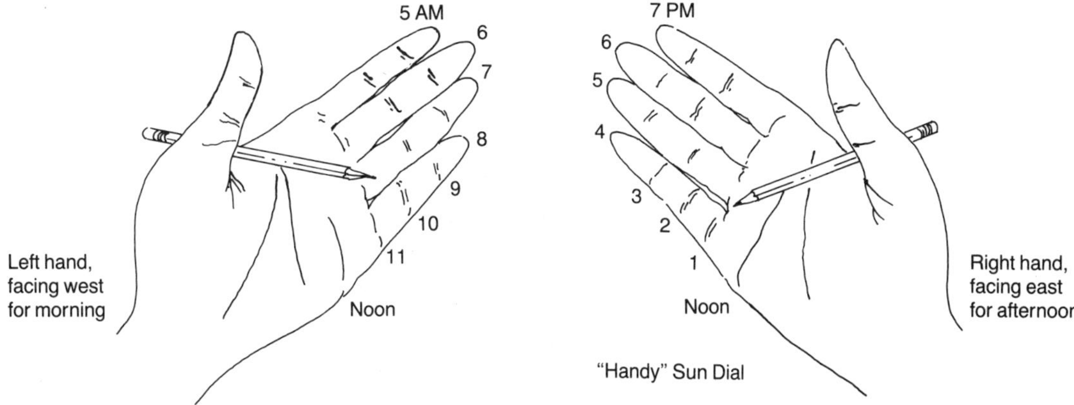

"Handy" Sun Dial

A Sundial in Your Hand

Everyone knows that the sun rises in the east, moves across the sky and sets in the west. And everyone knows that a sundial uses this motion of the sun to tell time. But did you know that you can make your hand into a sundial using nothing more than a pencil or pen?

If you want to know what time it is before noon, use your left hand. Tuck the pencil in between your thumb and the side of your hand. Hold the pencil so that it leans over your palm at an angle of about 45°. That is about halfway between lying flat and standing straight up. Finally, turn your hand so that your fingers point to the west.

Where does the pencil's shadow point? If it falls at the tip of your second finger (pointer), it is 5 A.M. The third fingertip indicates 6 A.M. and the fourth 7 A.M. The tip of your little finger is 8 A.M., the top crease is 9 A.M., the bottom crease is 10 A.M., and the base of the finger is 11 A.M. Noon is the top crease of your palm.

To tell the time after noon, use your right hand pointing to the east. The hours are as follows: noon at the top crease of your palm; 1 P.M. at the base of your little finger; 2 and 3 P.M. at the creases of that finger. And 4, 5, 6 and 7 P.M. are at the tip of the fifth, fourth, third and second fingers.

A Clock in the Sky

The sundial in your hand works very well during the daylight hours when the sun's light can cast a shadow. But how can you use the sky to tell the time at night, after the sun has set? There is a wonderfully simple clock in the sky that can give you the approximate time when it is dark outside.

The clock in the sky is the Little Dipper. Every night the Little Dipper appears to rotate around Polaris, the last star in its handle. The direction the cup is facing can give you a rough idea of the nighttime hours.

To use the clock in the sky, face north and find the Little Dipper. Then check the direction it is facing. The chart below will then help you to determine the hour.

During January and February, you notice, the cup is pointing down toward the horizon at 6 P.M.; at midnight it is facing nearly directly east; and at 6 A.M. it is facing up or overhead. Therefore, if on January 12th you see the cup halfway between the horizon and east, you know it's about 9 P.M., halfway between 6 P.M. and midnight. You can find the time on any other night in the year in the same way—as long as it is clear enough to see the Little Dipper.

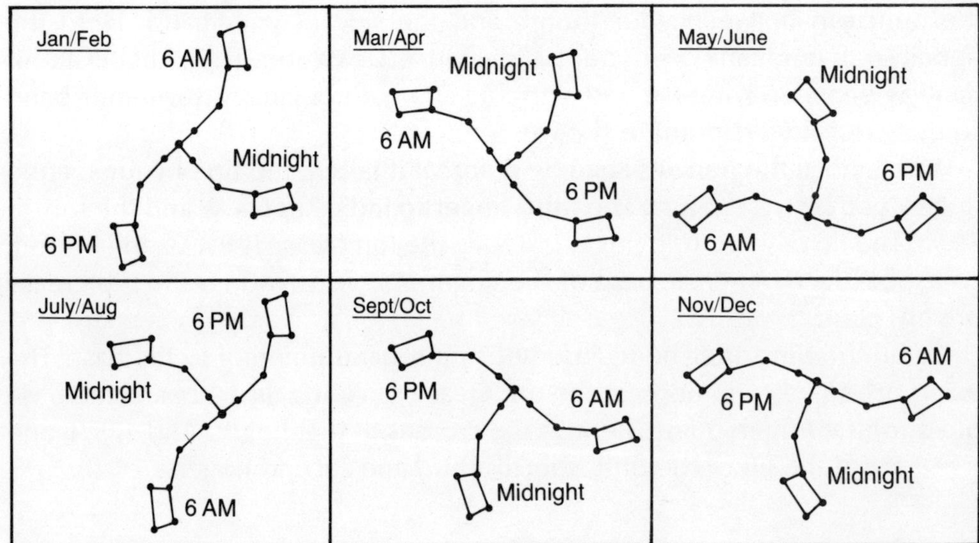

Telling Time by the Stars

The normal solar day is, of course, the 24 hours it takes for the earth to spin once on its axis. But because the earth also orbits around the sun as it spins on its axis, the length of the day in relation to the stars is not the same as the solar day. The time according to the stars is known as sidereal time.

As measured by the stars, the sun rises nearly 4 minutes later each day. Compared to a solar day, a sidereal day is only 23 hours, 56 minutes. That is because every day the earth moves a little along its orbit, and therefore has to spin a little farther to get back to where it was in relation to the sun.

The one day of the year that sidereal time and local solar time agree is on the autumn equinox, on or about September 22nd. But from then on every sidereal day is 4 minutes shorter than the solar day. Actually, in one year, sidereal time has gained a full day over solar time.

To find the sidereal time at any moment during the year, you must first figure out the number of days since September 22nd. You then add 4 minutes to the local time for every day. There is, however, a shortcut you can use for approximate figures. Four minutes a day works out to just under 30 minutes a week (7 days times 4 equals 28 minutes, which can be rounded off to 30 minutes), and 2 hours a month (30 days times 4 equals 120 minutes, or 2 hours).

For example, here's how you can calculate sidereal time at 9 A.M. on October 29th. It is one month and one week from September 22nd. Therefore, you add 2 hours for the month and 30 minutes for the week to arrive at 11:30 A.M. as the approximate sidereal time.

Can you figure out the sidereal time for today's date?

Constructing a Homemade Planetarium

A planetarium is a place where images of heavenly objects are projected on the inside of a large dome. To make your own planetarium, you'll need a flashlight (the largest one you have), a few shirt cardboards and two nails, one thin, the other slightly thicker.

Start by tracing circles the size of the flashlight lens on the cardboard.

Around each one, draw another circle about one inch beyond the original one. Fit as many as you can on the cardboard. Cut out the larger circles.

Next, draw the stars of a constellation within the inner circle. Write down the name of the constellation. Make some sort of special mark for the larger stars. With the thicker nail, punch holes in the cardboard for these stars. Punch holes for the other stars with the thinner nail.

Now hold one cardboard constellation centered over the lens of the flashlight. Turn the flashlight on. This works best in a dark room. Depending on the flashlight, you may be able to project the star image onto the ceiling or a blank wall. Does it look like the stars you see in the sky on a dark night?

Prepare five or ten different constellation images. Mix them up and hold them over the flashlight one at a time. Can you recognize all the constellations? Test your friends. See how many constellations they know.

In time, you'll find that the more activities you try and the more observations you make, the more you will enjoy gazing at the stars, tracking the comets and mapping the sky.

For Further Reading

• *On star gazing:*

Gallant, Roy A. *The Constellations.* New York: Four Winds, 1979.

Moore, Patrick. *Naked-Eye Astronomy.* New York: Norton, 1965.

Muirden, James. *The Amateur Astronomer's Handbook.* New York: Crowell, 1974 (revised ed.).

———*Astronomy Handbook.* New York: Arco, 1982.

Sherrod, P. Clay, and T. L. Koed. *A Complete Manual of Amateur Astronomy.* Englewood Cliffs, NJ: Prentice-Hall, 1981.

• *On comet tracking:*

Berger, Melvin. *Comets, Meteors and Asteroids.* New York: Putnam's, 1981.

Calder, Nigel. *The Comet is Coming.* New York: Viking, 1980.

Yeomans, Donald K. *The Comet Halley Handbook.* Washington, DC: Government Printing Office, 1981.

• *On sky mapping:*

Branley, Franklyn M. *Experiments in Sky Watching.* New York: Crowell, 1959.

Greenleaf, Peter. *Experiments in Space Science.* New York: Arco, 1980.

Jobb, Jamie. *The Night Sky Book.* Boston: Little, Brown, 1977.

Knox, Richard. *Experiments in Astronomy for Amateurs.* New York: St. Martin's, 1976.

• Leading astronomy magazines:

Astronomy
AstroMedia Corporation
625 E. St. Paul Avenue
P.O. Box 92788
Milwaukee, WI 53202

Sky and Telescope
Sky Publishing Company
49 Bay Street Road
Cambridge, MA 02238

• Monthly newsletter with current sky charts:

McDonald Observatory News
The University of Texas
McDonald Observatory
Room RLM 15.308
Austin, TX 78712

• For cassettes and maps for star gazing in each season, contact:

Astronomical Society of the Pacific
Tapes Department
1290 24th Avenue
San Francisco, CA 94122

• For information on observing Comet Halley, contact:

International Halley Watch
Jet Propulsion Laboratory
Mailstop T–1166
4800 Oak Grove Drive
Pasadena, CA 91109

Index